Making Boxes, Baskets & Bowls

Warren J. Asa

Sterling Publishing Co., Inc.   New York

Edited by Claire Bazinet

Library of Congress Cataloging-in-Publication Data

Asa, Warren J.
    Making boxes, baskets, & bowls / Warren J. Asa.
       p.   cm.
    Includes index.
    ISBN 0-8069-8260-8
    1. Woodwork.   2. Wooden boxes.   3. Bowls (Tableware).   4. Baskets.
 I. Title.   II. Title: Making boxes, baskets, and bowls.
TT180.A79   1992
674′.8—dc20
                                              92-25311
                                               CIP

10 9 8 7 6 5 4 3 2 1

Published in 1992 by Sterling Publishing Company, Inc.
387 Park Avenue South, New York, N.Y. 10016
© 1992 by Warren J. Asa
Distributed in Canada by Sterling Publishing
% Canadian Manda Group, P.O. Box 920, Station U
Toronto, Ontario, Canada M8Z 5P9
Distributed in Great Britain and Europe by Cassell PLC
Villiers House, 41/47 Strand, London WC2N 5JE, England
Distributed in Australia by Capricorn Link Ltd.
P.O. Box 665, Lane Cove, NSW 2066
Manufactured in the United States of America

Sterling ISBN 0-8069-8260-8

*This book is dedicated
to all craftworkers.*

*May you find ideas, instruction,
and inspiration in its pages.*

ACKNOWLEDGMENTS

Most authors begin their acknowledgments by thanking their families for putting up with their bad moods during the months they were holed up writing their books. My family had to deal with some of that, for which they do have my thanks. But when you write a craft book, your family is subjected to even more heinous treatment. My wife, Mary Jeanne, our children, Linda, Joe, and Bonnie, and our son-in-law, Ernie, have had to cope with wood soaking in the bathtub, cowhides being stretched in the backyard, the patio ankle-deep in shavings, and the top of our motor home looking like a pile of driftwood when we returned from trips. There may have been a few groans along the way but they all kept their sense of humor and survived in good order. Moreover, they were not simply passive observers but contributed by offering suggestions, posing for and taking photos, and actually helping on a few projects.

My special thanks to Mary Jeanne for proofreading my work and trying to keep my grammar on track.

Other thanks must go back many years to my parents, Clarence and Helen Asa, who always encouraged me in my craft endeavors. To my shop teachers, Wayne Yonker and E. J. Harrison, and my blacksmithing mentors, William and Oscar Maisch, I owe my gratitude for many hours of patient coaching. Lola Elliott, my art teacher in the seventh and eighth grades, taught me in that short time what I know about color and line and inspired me to continue to broaden my horizons. Another positive force in my life was Dr. Harry Fuller, Professor of Botany at the University of Illinois, who encouraged me to travel and to never stop learning.

In more recent years, I would like to acknowledge my gratitude to Mike Rubel for the use of his blacksmithing facilities, for his home for photo backgrounds, and for his critiques of my work.

Finally, I wish also to thank *Boys' Life, Popular Woodworking,* and *Woodwork* magazines for their cooperation in the use of some projects that first appeared in their pages.

CONTENTS

BOWLS 113

WOODCRAFTING

AN INTRODUCTION

Making Boxes, Baskets & Bowls is both an idea book and a how-to-do-it book. It consists of this introductory chapter, which I hope you will read before starting any of the projects, and four sections that stand alone—you need not approach them in order. Reading my remarks and the technical notes given at the beginning of each section will, however, stand you in good stead and give you an appreciation of the various crafts.

I hope the dozens of projects in this book and their many variations will inspire you to try several things you feel you just have to make. My aim was to cover some of the better-known items in each of the four categories, including bucket

making (cooperage), and then go farther afield. Some readers may feel that I've included too much odd stuff but I suspect others will find these unique projects the best part of the book. What's an idea book for if not to stretch your imagination and offer up some new craft horizons.

In keeping with the "how-to" goals of this book I have included text, photos, and drawings of almost every project and endeavored to give complete, though often brief, working instructions.

Every art-craft book has to zero in on a target audience. A book for beginners deals mainly with the basics, and usually gets into few projects. On

the other hand, a volume aimed at experts may end up dealing primarily with theory and the philosophy of the discipline under discussion, again missing the heart of the matter—projects. My target readers are in the middle; those who know how to use their tools, can take accurate measurements and read plans, and who love to work on projects. That's what this book concentrates on, ideas and directions for making things.

How does anyone come to write a book about fabricating boxes, bowls, buckets, and baskets? I don't have a precise answer but I've always found containers to be so marvelously practical. This was true of my first tool chest, the wire basket that fastened to the handlebars of the bike I rode as a teen, and of the rucksack I carried in the Mountain Troops. Then, sometime in my life, I began to realize that there could be great beauty in containers like the beaded pipe bags of the Plains Indians, the sandalwood boxes of the Orient, and the finely woven baskets of the California Indians. When I started doing freelance writing a high percentage of my craft articles dealt with the making of containers so a book about them seemed to be a natural.

"SPECIAL" PROJECTS

Naturally, with my varied interests, I have included a broad scope of projects in this volume. The largest and smallest items are both boxes, namely the Stamp Caddy and the Blanket Chest.

My nominees for projects with the oddest names are the Small Carved Bowl called a noggin, the Milk Piggin, and the Firkin. The project that stands out as the one you will most likely spend hours playing with is the skittles game. And finally, which of the projects do I consider the most unique? My answer would have to be the Indian Box and the Partitioned Bowl. There are many other handsome and functional projects but I am hoping that my mentioning these few will whet your creative appetites and get you excited about getting in the shop and making the chips fly.

The projects that I most enjoy making in quantity for gifts are the Stamp and Bottle Caddies, Weed Pots, and Bentwood Boxes. Many of the handmade projects from this book are regularly used outside of our home. Of these I have had the most favorable comments on the Picnic Baskets and the Lunch Box.

My nominees for projects with the oddest names are the Small Carved Bowl called a noggin, the Milk Piggon, and the Firkin. The project that stands out as the one you will most likely spend hours playing with is the skittles game. And finally, which of the projects do I consider the most unique? My answer would have to be the Indian Box and the Partitioned Bowl. There are many other handsome and functional projects but I am hoping that my mentioning these few will whet your creative appetites and get you excited about getting in the shop and making the chips fly.

Indian Boxes are one of the most unique and colorful containers you can make.

WOODS AND WOODWORKING

North America has a wonderful woodworking heritage that started with the native Americans and was broadened and enriched by ideas from Africa, Asia, Europe, as well as the countries to the south, and the Pacific islands. We have inherited these centuries of wood lore and that is in a way a heavy responsibility. This knowledge should not be lost but passed on to as yet unborn generations and most certainly to our children.

There is a genuine warmth and beauty in wood. It's fun to work, the results of its workings are useful, and it has an age-old appeal that has not been pushed aside by glass, chrome, or plastic. Many of the projects in this book are time-consuming. But if you craft them carefully you will have a thing of functional beauty that will last for generations. To spend hours making a simple item of wood may strike some efficiency-minded executives as the height of folly, but the folly of many business practices can also be questioned.

Some may view my penchant for hand tools as antiquated and full of nostalgia and I readily admit that if you wanted to make a profit crafting any of these projects you would have to streamline my procedures. However, I enjoy making the chips fly with hand tools so I do encourage their use especially for novice shop workers. Also, if we truly want a cleaner, healthier world it is certainly better for us to burn off some of our cholesterol rather than constantly calling on the grid for more kilowatts which only adds to pollution and depletes irreplaceable fossil fuels.

I especially like to make projects from scratch even to the extent of harvesting the oak splits, willow twigs, burls, or birchbark directly from nature. This, too, takes time but it adds an outdoor element to shopwork that I like. Perhaps an experience from my youth will illustrate my desire to work from scratch.

While in high school I was the handicraft instructor at our council Scout camp for two summers. Precut wallet kits, a rather new item, proved quite popular at some camps. One day, a professional Scouter visiting our camp dropped by the craft shop. He asked how many wallets had been made. I gave him a figure. "How come so few?" he wanted to know. I showed him our calfskins and cowhides. He was amazed that every leather project our campers made had to be planned, measured, cut, punched, and laced by the individual Scout. It was the same with metalwork, where we had sheet copper, tin snips, jeweler's saws, and solder. True, our campers produced fewer projects, but what they made was *really* their creation since they had to learn and perform every process needed to complete it.

After telling you how much I enjoy working with hand tools I feel I must state that I do have power tools in my shop. The efficiency, accuracy, and clean cuts of power tools are essential in a production shop and mighty handy for the hobbyist. My principal power tools consist of a table saw-joiner combination, a Shopsmith which I use mainly as a lathe, a band saw, drill press, disk sander, and bench grinder. Portable power tools include a belt sander, drill, sabre saw, small rotary tool, and a flex shaft tool. Just a word on my hand tools. In some of the pictures you may notice some old and odd-looking tools. No, these are not antiques, although I allow that some of my tools have a few years on them, but rather tools that I have made. Mine is not a mass-production shop nor have I ever been involved with a commercial shop. I suspect if I had been, I would have never become interested in so many crafts and this book would have never been written.

I like to think that every woodworker is entitled to a philosophy on the subject. To me eighty percent of proper woodworking is accuracy of cut. Whether you are handsawing a board to length or trimming off its edges on a table saw you want the length and width to be correct. It's the same when chiselling out dovetail or mortise joints. Some cuts are more critical but almost all are important. The other twenty percent of the job is turning in screws, applying glue, clamping, and finishing, which are also important in producing a fine project. So, measure twice before you cut, and be sure your tools are sharp and that you know how to use them. If you lack the hand—eye coordination necessary to do certain jobs, keep trying. The saying "Practice makes perfect" has a lot of truth in it.

While on the subject of philosophy, I would like to toss in my thoughts on design. Although I don't look upon myself as a rebel in society, I do admit to having a rebellious philosophy when it comes to design. Invariably I seek ways to make things simpler, prettier, or different. Why make a thing different? Partly to make it individually yours and partly just as an experiment to see if the new method is more efficient or better-looking. Obviously if you are copying an established style, you must keep to that style, but there still may be construction techniques that can be altered. I won't say I always succeed with my innovations but I enjoy trying, and I hope you will try your own hand at designing. Perhaps the varied projects in this book will be the leavening to get your imagination rising into high gear.

And while on the topic of design I might as well have my say about what is pleasing and what is not. "Beauty is in the eye of the beholder," goes the old saying. Some may view my designs as too squat and bulky and others may see them as too tall and slim. Still others may think my chests too tall or my baskets too wide. To all of these I can only say I followed my eye and instinct to make what, to me, was the most aesthetically pleasing design possible. If you see things differently please change the size and shape to suit yourself. As another old saying goes, "One person's junk is another person's treasure."

I think I should confess to a pet peeve about woodworking, and that is the wasting of wood. True, wood is a renewable resource but trees take time to grow, and first have to be planted. When I pass a landfill dump and see trucks waiting to dump hundreds of board feet of lumber, I cringe. Certainly, the answers to burying our scrap are not simple, but there must be alternatives to this wasting and depletion of our natural resources—solutions that will benefit us and our children.

Some may say, "But we only have a small home shop. What can we do?" Everyone who works wood can make a difference. If we are all frugal in our use of forest products we can make a tremendous difference. I would like to tell you about some of the ways I save wood, and some other conservation stories I have heard.

As I engage in a broad spectrum of woodworking activities it's easy for me to save short ends from the large projects for use on the smaller ones. I find that even small blocks can become useful for projects like the salt and pepper shakers and stamp caddy in the Boxes section or the Indian bowl. Really tiny pieces of choice woods have value for jewelry making. If you don't engage in this craft, pass your scrap on to a club or individual who does. Stuff that is absolutely scrap I burn in the barbecue in place of charcoal and the ashes go in the compost. My plane shavings are collected to start fires in the forge and all the sawdust and chips go on the compost pile. I believe I can honestly say that almost nothing is wasted in my shop.

Much of the wood I use is salvaged from pallets, crates, and other sources where it was slated to be burned or buried. Not only does this save a natural resource but I often get the material by trading a few home-crafted items, which is a real bargain for me. Sometimes when I'm ready to start a project I discover that my recycled wood is the wrong size. I never alter the proportions in the design but I often alter the size to utilize the stock I have on hand.

Over the years I have run into a number of ways of using wood to its fullest potential. I'd like to share a few of these with you. One lumberyard that I deal with gives all of its chips to a local gardener who composts them. In turn, the gardener makes sure that the yard's counters and office have fresh flowers. Another yard donates all of its cut-offs to the junior high shop classes. One of my friends does most of his craft work with mill ends passed on to him by a local cabinet shop, and another friend panelled a room in his home with attractive squares of ash plywood. He made the squares from the window cut-outs of a motorhome manufacturer.

One of the most original tales of utilizing wood that would have otherwise ended up as chips was told by California furniture maker Sam Maloof during one of his lectures. If you know his creations you know that he often puts items together with countersunk sheet-metal screws and covers the holes with contrasting wooden plugs. He mentioned the high cost of the wood for these plugs to one of his professional wood-turning friends one day and the friend replied that he regularly turned bowls from such woods. The result was that the friend now works over the interior of his bowl blanks with a plug cutter and it's easy to guess who gets the plugs. If we could all be this creative we could surely make a dent in the world demand for wood.

SAFETY

A few of you may feel like skipping this section, figuring that you've already read more about safety over the years than you ever wanted to know. I suggest you don't. The few minutes it takes to read it may save you a finger or an eye.

Most woodworkers look upon hand tools as friends and I agree with that, but a saw or chisel carelessly used can cause a mean wound. I learned the fine points of ax use from an old mountain man in New Mexico who had a rule for using an ax that holds true for most hand tools.

Doc Loomis put it this way: "Be sure you know what you will hit if you miss what you are aiming at." In his case it reminded him to get his foot out from behind the log he was chopping. In the case of a woodworker it means to get your hand away from any piece you are sawing or carving.

My favorite saying about the machines in my shop is, "Power tools have no friends." If you get zapped by a power tool it will keep taking bites until you can pull free or shut the thing down. A woodworker I know was using his table saw when his little finger hit the blade. With luck this might have resulted in only a cut finger but the saw blade flipped his hand over, took off the thumb, and chewed up the other fingers as well.

Another safety concept that holds true for both hand and power tools is, "Be aware of the cutting edge." Whether you are whittling, operating a drill press, or using the band saw the cutting edge is the point of danger. And, conversely, tools that we don't think of as having a cutting edge, like a screwdriver, can still draw blood if used carelessly.

The good Lord gave us only two eyes and it is up to us to protect and preserve them. I like large, full-face masks because they offer good protection and don't interfere with my spectacles. Other possibilities for eye protection are goggles, half-masks, and, for those who don't wear glasses, tempered safety spectacles. Eye-protection devices are of no value if they aren't used so be sure yours is close at hand and kept clean. When a face mask gets grimy, resist the urge to wipe it with your hand or a shop rag. The chances of scratching the plastic are great. It's much better to wash the mask with running water and, if it's really dirty, use warm water and soap.

Every once in a while when I am in a hurry I find myself doing a job while still holding the tool from the last task. This is a dangerous practice that I have to work to overcome. A related topic is how to safely carry a tool. There seems to be no overall rule on this but the general consensus seems to be to carry tools at your side with the cutting edge held away from the body and in such a manner that the tool can be discarded safely if you should fall.

Another major item in safety are human factors such as fatigue, boredom, excitement, and anger. Thinking people would not start a long auto trip if they were extremely tired nor should they operate power tools when in that condition. However, fatigue can creep up on a person so be aware that you may not be as alert at the end of a long day of shop work as you were at the start.

A good analogy of how boredom affects shop safety is that of a pilot making a solo flight. We hear of few accidents on solo flights but many more on subsequent flights when pilots have more experience. Why should that be? Probably because a novice pilot is on a natural high for the first spin and concentrates on doing everything right. As flying becomes routine the chances of the pilot becoming complacent and letting attention wander are greater. So if you are doing a repetitious shop job, especially one involving power tools, take frequent breaks and do everything you can to maintain your concentration.

Distractions can take many forms like a baseball hit through a shop window, the wind suddenly blowing a door closed, or even a person's noisy entry. Some people react with a startle to such surprises, while others don't blink an eye. If you fit in the former group, it's best to plan power-tool jobs when no one is likely to disturb you.

For whatever reason, people do at times get angry and distraught. This is no time to do any tricky shop procedure. To do so is to fly in the face of reason. Anger or stress can warp reason and you don't want to be in that condition when fingers and eyes are at stake. Make it a rule to stay out of the shop until you calm down. If your rebuttal is that you use woodworking as therapy to help you calm down I can only suggest that you stay away from power tools when you are agitated and concentrate on such danger-proof tasks as hand sanding.

Physical elements within the shop that promote safety include good lighting, a clean floor, and uncluttered bench tops and work areas. Loud noise is another shop hazard that can be countered with earmuff-type hearing protectors. A well-ventilated area is suggested when working with solvents and finishes, but you will probably also want to wear a respirator. Be sure the one you select is rated to filter out the vapors from whatever you are using. As every woodworker knows, sanding dust is a major shop pollutant. Many dust-removal systems are now on the market and many craftworkers have designed and built their own setups. Dust masks are also highly desirable. And don't forget to wear hand and eye protection when working with caustic substances.

Fire safety is an area that is often overlooked in the shop. If you use a soldering iron or torch, do your work on a fireproof surface like a layer of bricks. Keep your electrical wiring up to code and replace frayed extension cords. Equipping your shop with a smoke detector and a fire extinguisher are absolute musts. I recommend the ABC dry chemical-type extinguisher that will deal with burning solids, liquids, and electrical fires. Lastly, keep your shop clean and neat so there isn't unnecessary fuel for a fire.

Keeping tools sharp and in good repair is just practicing that old saw "A stitch in time saves nine." Failure to repair a loose hammerhead resulting in a broken window or worse is no way to operate a shop. And how about keeping logical guards in place and using push sticks? All good ideas meant to protect you. I have a personal rule about push sticks that I try never to break. Whenever I am pushing boards through a power tool on a table, I will push with my hands only up to the table edge and then switch to a push stick.

An ever-changing source of potential danger in the shop is the use of chemicals. You might say that can't apply to you because you don't use anything really toxic or caustic. Many woodworkers don't realize it but some people are allergic to very common items like turpentine and the things that are added to linseed oil to make it into the product we call boiled linseed oil.

This is such a complex and changing field that the product that is thought safe today may be tomorrow's villain. I can only suggest a few simple guidelines. If you show any reaction to a chemical, like sneezing, runny nose, watering eyes, skin rash, or headaches, discontinue using it and check with the manufacturer about your problem. It might be that you will be able to use this item by wearing gloves or a respirator. If you have a serious reaction to a product, such as dizziness, shortness of breath, irregular heartbeat, or damage to skin tissue, leave your shop immediately and seek medical assistance. Woodworkers should also be aware that the sawdust from certain woods can cause individuals to have allergic reactions. Information on shop allergies and toxic substances is constantly becoming available so read current woodworking periodicals for the latest reports.

I am right-handed and I find that my left hand receives the lion's share of cuts and scrapes. This may not appear logical but, when you think about it, it makes sense because my right hand is safely holding a hammer, saw, or chisel handle while my left is out there where danger lurks. Is there a lesson in this for us? You bet there is. It's simply to keep the hand that doesn't appear to be doing any work out of harm's way. Remember Doc Loomis's rule. And, speaking of hands, have you noticed that right-handed workers wear out their left gloves first, and vice versa for southpaws?

To wear or not to wear gloves during woodworking is a question that is sometimes asked. Some people never wear them claiming they are unsafe. I wear them in the shop for a few jobs like pushing splintery wood through a table saw or while doing the rough work on a large lathe project. I prefer leather gloves that fit tightly over the hands. The ones I use have either a tight-fitting knit top long enough to go under my shirt sleeve or a stiff gauntlet that extends well beyond the wrist. I look for protection from any source of danger and find that gloves prevent many scrapes and burns. Can gloves get caught in machinery? They sure can, but so can shirt sleeves and tails. We don't take our shirts off to do shop work, we just make sure that they are out of harm's way so do the same whenever you wear gloves.

Whenever I hear of a shop accident I inquire about the details. Some of the stories are bloody and I'll not sicken you with them but they do make the point that woodworking can be dangerous and should be approached with intelligence and caution. In this very unscientific sampling I have come to the conclusion that table and radial arm saws are the power tools most likely to be involved in an accident. Perhaps this is because these tools are so widely used or because they are used on repetitive jobs or because they are so efficient we tend to become overconfident when using them but they are real finger-stealers so treat them with the same respect you would a caged tiger.

If you really work at safety you should be able to enjoy your shop for many years with only the occasional scratch. If you find that you regularly get hurt or become ill while doing woodworking I would suggest you step back and take a critical look at your entire setup. The problem might be too high or low a workbench, poor lighting or dust control, or a host of other things. But take time to track them down and correct them. Woodworking should be fun and I'm sure you want it to be so make shop safety your highest priority. Just as "Eternal vigilance is the price of freedom" so eternal safety vigilance is the price we pay for an accident-free shop.

THE PROJECTS

I selected, designed, and personally constructed all of the projects in this book. My wish is that you, in turn, make a bunch of them. Members of my family helped me put long boards through my table saw but on only two projects did I receive any physical help. My son Joe assisted me on two of the box projects.

I cannot and don't wish to take credit for the original concept of all these projects. What I did was design and draw plans for the projects I made. Many of the ideas came from traditional Native American crafts, or things made by our hardy pioneer ancestors, or from other cultures around the world. On just a few like the Lunch Box, Lantern Case, and Kyack Box-table can I lay any claim to originality.

Let me emphasize how important it is to study the drawings and photos before you start a project. I have tried to place simpler projects at the beginning of the sections so if you decide to start with a project near the end of a chapter you might do well to review the previous projects.

A pair of Kyack Boxes set up as a table at Supai Canyon, Arizona.

The how-to photographs in this book are accurate records of how I handled certain steps of construction. The majority of the photos were taken on my patio in natural sunlight. In addition, almost every project in *Making Boxes, Baskets & Bowls* is accompanied by one or more freehand drawings which I have attempted to make as accurate as possible. Important hidden elements are shown as dotted lines and center lines are indicated with a series of dots and long dashes. Quite often I have simplified the drawings by not showing all of the hidden lines or by using cross-sectional drawings.

Most of the drawings include dimensions, given in feet and inches. Here, again, I have endeavored to be accurate but, as I use a lot of hand-planed lumber that is not consistent in thickness, some of the figures may not always "add up." Let me say, too, that the dimensions given here don't indicate that they are the best size for a project. If you wish to make your version larger or smaller I say go to it.

I have attempted, in all of the drawings, to show you the shape of the completed project as well as the important construction details. In a few projects I have included different ways of doing things to show the many options that are available to you. Some drawings also include ornamentation other than that seen in the photos. Again, I did this purposely to make you aware of various design possibilities.

GATHERING CRAFT MATERIAL

A tramp in the mountains or a walk by the seashore are both pleasant and they can provide material for shopwork. But everyone must be aware that few things today are free and that laws vary tremendously from area to area. If you own a wood lot or a piece of timberland consider yourself lucky and practice good husbandry on the bit of nature that has been allotted to you. My definition of conservation is not the non-use of natural resources but the wise use. If you don't own land, your safest bet is to look for native materials in areas where you have the owner's permission. The following paragraphs deal with the specifics of collecting craft materials during outings.

Logs, burls, and roots for box making or for turning can be had from many sources. A neighbor cuts down a tree, a city crew trims some big branches, or a contractor clears land for a development and you have valuable craft material for the asking. Keep your eyes open for such finds but always ask permission before taking anything. Quite often the workers will be eager to assist you because you save them the job of carting the stuff away. I've even had them ask me how long I would like the logs cut. However, it's a good idea to carry a big-toothed tree-trimming saw in your vehicle to cut the logs to length in case no one volunteers to do it for you.

Tree Bark

Birch bark for boxes and baskets can be gleaned from trees felled for lumber or cleared for roadways or building sites. The bark from logs cut for firewood and left on a woodpile for a few years can still be used by soaking it in water for two or three days. Never cut bark from standing trees. This does not automatically kill the tree, as you are only removing the outer layer of bark not the vital inner phloem tissue, but it does make the tree more susceptible to disease and to drying out and it renders the birch tree unsightly. So never let it be said that a woodworker created this mischief in the name of art.

The technical aspects of harvesting oak splits and ash splints are covered in the chapter on basketry. Again let me emphasize the importance of only cutting material on private property where you have the owner's permission. The myriad other basket-making materials, like pine needles, corn husks, grain straw, and swamp and prairie grass, can often be had for the asking and gathering.

Modern Birch-Bark Box with Southwest Indian designs.

Beach Wood

Saltwater beaches can offer the shopworker roots, logs, odd-shaped branches, and even lumber. Usually this is considered flotsam and jetsam and no one minds if you pick it up. However, there may well be laws somewhere that place restrictions on this, so check before gathering. Along freshwater lakes and rivers, I would definitely ascertain if it's okay to glean before picking up anything. I'll end this brief discussion on gathering wild materials with a story about how I acquired some fine pieces of oak.

Some years back I organized an American Youth Hostel raft trip on the Klamath River in northern California. During the trip I kept finding nice oak barrel staves washed up on the sand bars. My mother raised no fools, so I gathered these up and placed them in our spacious rafts. At a stop I asked a local resident why there were so many barrel staves in the river. He told me that, some years before, a still was located in the woods by the river. Every time the still was raided by the T-men the moonshiners got rid of the evidence, the filled barrels, by rolling them into the river. Without this evidence, they could not be prosecuted. I've often wondered since what the fish and river otters thought was happening, especially when the barrels eventually broke open.

METHODS OF WORKING WITH WOOD

Shaping and Hollowing

The shaping of complex curves, like those forming the Pirate Chest project in the boxes section, can be done with a number of tools. You don't need to purchase them all, as one or two will usually do the job. For the first rough work the adz and drawknife are ideal. Follow up with straight gouges, scorp, and inshave. Finishing work is best done with tools that provide a controlled cut, like standard and curved spokeshaves and curved bottom carving planes. The latter tool comes in both a push and pull model. I have a slight personal preference for the push type but they are both wonderful tools for this task. The handles of a spokeshave preclude their being used in tight spots but then the carving plane comes to the rescue. The final work on these complex curves can be accomplished with curved scrapers and abrasive paper wrapped around rubber sanding blocks.

My favorite tools for hollowing out cavities are the small adz, inshave, scorp, crooked knife, and gouges, especially the bent and spoon designs. I'm not speaking here of hollowing out a bowl on the lathe, but rather making carved bowls and the like. If practical I like to first drill out the cavity with spade, Forstner or brad point bits. Plan your drilling carefully lest you go a bit too deep and mar the sides of the project. Large rotary burrs like the "wood hog" might be the answer for some big jobs. Tools like the adz and scorp were well known 150 years ago. They are less known now but they are still available.

To finish the inside of these cavities I use curved scrapers and hand sanding. A portable drill with a flexible rubber disk covered with abrasive paper in its chuck can also be a big help. A small, shop-made version of this is described in the Partitioned Bowl project. This small sanding disk has many applications in finishing petite articles. Many variations of this sanding rig can be crafted in your shop when the need arises.

I want to mention one more favorite tool, although it has nothing to do with shaping or hollowing. This is the scissors-like tool called craft shears. Available at leather craft stores, the shears are a delight for cutting rattan, oak splits, leather, and even thin wood. You might think that a very sharp pair of tin snips or heavy-duty scissors will do just as well, but after trying craft shears you will never use the other tools again.

Bending Wood

In every section except the one on bowls there are some projects that require wood to be bent. If you have crafted snowshoes, a fish-landing net, or a kayak you are an old hand at this method of shaping wood. If not, the whole idea may strike you as a bit frightening. Fear not, it's not as hard as it looks. You will likely ruin a few pieces, but that won't be the end of the world.

A few readers may have access to a steam box. For the majority who don't, I'll provide a few tips on bending wood without exotic equipment. I divide bending into two categories. The first I call light-duty bending. The material used in this is quite thin, usually less than $\frac{1}{8}$ of an inch thick, and normally will not require steaming. If I am dealing with long pieces, I cover them with hot water in the bathtub. After a day in this water, the pieces are usually flexible enough to bend into a circle that will fit into a sink. Give them two or three soaks of an hour's duration each in the hottest tap water available. This is normally enough preparation to do light bending. I keep the wood submerged with chunks of stainless steel. Whatever you use, be sure that it won't rust and stain the wood. If your wood doesn't appear flexible enough after this treatment, you can bring into play some of the techniques in the following paragraph.

For heavy-duty bending, a steam box is of course ideal but, lacking one, this is my procedure. The candidates for this treatment are often long so I drop them in a section of steel pipe that is capped on one end and pour in boiling water. To keep the pieces submerged I close the end with a wooden plug. I repeat this process until I can bend the pieces enough to fit inside a large pot with some water. Shorter pieces of wood can go directly into the pot. Sometimes I allow the wood to rest in the water and other times I keep it above the water.

If the wood is in the water, I allow it to simmer until flexible enough for my purposes. If the wood is elevated above the water, I bring the water to a boil with a lid on the pot and steam the wood until it's bendable. Use tongs and wear heavy gloves when you remove a piece of wood to test it for flexibility. (A different method of steaming wood is given, in the Indian Box project section, on page 42.)

If the wood does not bend sufficiently for my purposes I place it back in the pot for more treatment. If it still resists bending, I try scraping the stiff areas with a regular glue scraper. This removes some wood but more than that the scraping seems to compress the wood fibres and this flattening definitely encourages the wood to be more flexible. Another idea is to grasp the piece in gloved hands and to flex it back and forth using careful and controlled hand movements. This has the effect of loosening the fibres, which again makes for greater flexibility. Lastly, you may have to actually thin the piece with a plane, spokeshave, or knife to make it bendable enough for your project. If after trying all the above without success, I would suggest a different piece of wood or perhaps a different species. My favorite woods for bending are white oak, ash, and American holly. Other woods for bending include elm, hackberry, maple, alder, and yellow cedar. Pieces for bending must have absolutely straight grain and be as free from flaws as possible. It is so important to have straight-grained wood for bending that a good argument can be made for splitting pieces for this purpose. These pieces that you rive out will have perfectly straight grain, but the pieces themselves may not be straight so splitting is not always the answer.

When you find you can bend the wood to your satisfaction you will probably need a form and some method to secure the piece around this form. I find I can usually make my forms from scrap wood. The bent piece is held in place with clamps, rope, or cord. Even heavy rubber bands work for small projects.

It is not uncommon for steamed pieces to twist or "cup" during drying. So make your forms as complete as possible and use plenty of clamps to try to prevent this. If the piece does warp a bit, it may not make any difference if the piece is a handle for a rustic basket. In fact, that could contribute to the character of the basket. However, in some cases this warping may present a problem. Quite often the piece can be straightened out with clamp pressure when it is glued in place. If this cannot be done it can be resoaked, bent around the form, and clamped even more carefully than before. Another possibility that may work, if the piece is thick enough, is to scrape or plane the warp out.

My normal procedure is to allow bent pieces to stay clamped for 24 hours. If the wood is still damp, I remove it from the form and hold it in the bent position with clamps or rope for another day. Next I check for fit and take any corrective action deemed necessary. Then the bent piece can be glued in place with yellow glue, or resorcinol if it will be used around water. When the glue is dry any excess can be scraped off and the piece sanded as needed.

Sanding and Finishing

How much to sand a project is an oft debated subject. My thinking is that the history and nature of the item under consideration should be the deciding factor. A rustic noggin or carved Indian bowl is traditionally completed with tool marks in evidence. The same may be true for basket handles and rims. The Mayan bowl is a turning project that features a tool-mark finish. At the other extreme are the turned bowls that are normally sanded to at least a 600-grit fineness, possibly even finer, and then polished to a fare-thee-well. The majority of the box projects in this book fall between these two extremes, having been sanded with 200- to 400-grit paper. Many of the coopered projects and some of the boxes were not sanded at all, having been completed with a sharp plane taking extremely light cuts. A well-tuned plane can take off shavings of a thickness of only one or two thousandths of an inch, leaving a surface that cannot be improved with abrasive paper. If you have not tried this technique, sharpen up your plane and do some experimenting on nice hard woods. I think you will be pleasantly surprised at the results.

In general, I find sanding less interesting than other woodworking jobs so I suspect I give it a lower priority. I do understand its importance but to me it is not a very creative task and one that I am most happy to complete and be done with.

For a detailed account of my methods of wood finishing, see the technical notes in the bowls section of this book.

FINAL THOUGHTS

The projects for this book have been built over a span of 40-plus years and the actual writing has occupied over two years. A lot of sweat, a few drops of blood, but no tears have gone into the work as it has been throughout an enjoyable labor of love. The dozens of projects will provide you with a myriad of things to make and perhaps these last remarks will give you a few things to think about.

In case you do not notice, I want to point out that not a single project here employs copper wire. This means that they don't require batteries or to be plugged into an electrical outlet to function. Whether you look upon the many electrical devices that have infiltrated our lives as banes or boons is up to you. But I like to think that this book and its projects harken back to a simpler age when the pace of life was slower, when excellent craft work and the people who did it were appreciated, and when things were made to last.

I imagine everyone has heard various sayings about being closer to God when working in a garden. As I like gardening, I can relate to them.

But, as a woodworker, I feel closest to God when I make the shaving curl off a piece of wood, one of the Almighty's choicest creations.

Finally, a phrase I came across recently, "the music of our hands," seems very appropriate for this book and the various crafts that it embraces. If we, through the music of our hands, create useful things that we pass on to family and friends, we are making the world a more loving place. If we craft some of these items from material that would otherwise be wasted, we are making the world a more sustainable place. And, if we fabricate projects of true beauty, I am sure we are making the world a better place.

My hope is that I have been able to convey in this volume some of my enthusiasm for working wood. For me the sheer enjoyment of crafting wood is hard to beat and I'm happy doing honorable work. I can do no better here than to wish you the same.

BOXES

Boxes, chests, and trunks have been important to mankind ever since we ceased being hunter-gatherers, discovered agriculture, started living in villages, and began acquiring an abundance of "stuff." Enter a Navajo hogan and you will find a circle of small trunks against the wall for personal and family possessions. Walk through a marketplace in Kenya and observe the stacks of rather flat boxes that are used to store everything from food to tools. Visit a nautical museum and there will be examples of seamen's chests. And what do we see inside the covered wagon in displays about the American West but a rawhide-covered trunk. Boxes and their kin are one of the most practical and logical of containers and their use is worldwide.

With boxes of so many sizes, shapes, and styles, the scope of this section is far-ranging. It includes utilitarian items like lunch, bread, and tool boxes as well as luxury boxes inlaid with silver. Here, too, are large chests weighing close to one hundred pounds and a tiny stamp caddy that tips the scale at but a few ounces. The two bentwood boxes that are covered expose a craftworker to some rather unusual techniques. The construction methods, materials, and forms of decoration are as varied as this broad subject.

I don't remember the first box I made but I imagine it was a rather crude affair hammered together with nails from salvaged orange crates. I do remember an early project that I called a camping box which served me well for many years. No, I didn't lash it to a packboard and carry it into the woods. Rather it was meant for trips where our duffel was transported by truck or trailer. It offered good protection during transit, organized storage in camp, and could be pressed into service as a seat or table when needed. I made it from ⅜-inch plywood and waterproofed it with layer after layer of oil paint. It had handles on both ends for carrying and a hasp for locking. For youth groups or large families this sort of box still has merit. It can be stacked during transit, provides secure storage at the destination, and can be decorated in an individual manner for instant recognition.

The projects that pass muster under the term box include chests, cases, and trunks. I always thought the term "trunk" odd until I saw a marvelous group of dioramas at a London museum showing human progress starting with the Stone Age. The first diorama of interest here showed the interior of a primitive dwelling of an early agricultural people. These village dwellers had things to store, and a hollowed-out section of tree trunk that looked a bit like a square-ended dugout canoe served as the container. Subsequent displays followed the evolution of the trunk through the Bronze and Iron ages where it acquired square sides, a hinged lid, a lock, and decorations. So the term "trunk" is not odd at all but comes directly from the original source.

More so than any of the other chapters this one is largely straightforward woodworking with flat sides and square corners, but look out for a few curves—like the pirate chest with the undulating lid. There are also a couple of round and oval shapes to challenge you. I like to encourage craftworkers to extend themselves and try new things and this chapter is no exception. You will also be exposed here to handcrafting hardware, covering projects with leather, and inlaying box lids with metal.

For all-around yeoman's service it's hard to find a container that offers more value than a box. Whether you decide to make an elegant jewelry receptacle, a destruction-proof toy box, or a knockabout tool chest I hope you have fun making it and I know you will enjoy the finished product, partly because it's useful and partly because it was your own creation. My final ode to the box is, "Be it ever so humble, there is no place like it for storing our junk and treasure."

TECHNICAL NOTES

Box Construction

A number of construction methods were employed in making these boxes. Some of the largest as well as a few small ones were put together by what I call the "six-board method"; that is, a separate board or panel is used for front, back, ends, top, and bottom. This seems like such a logical approach to box construction that it's easy to think that this method would dominate the chapter but such is not the case. Two rather different boxes are made with the bandsaw and table saw. These methods lend themselves better to small projects but many variations are possible. Bending enters the picture with the Bentwood

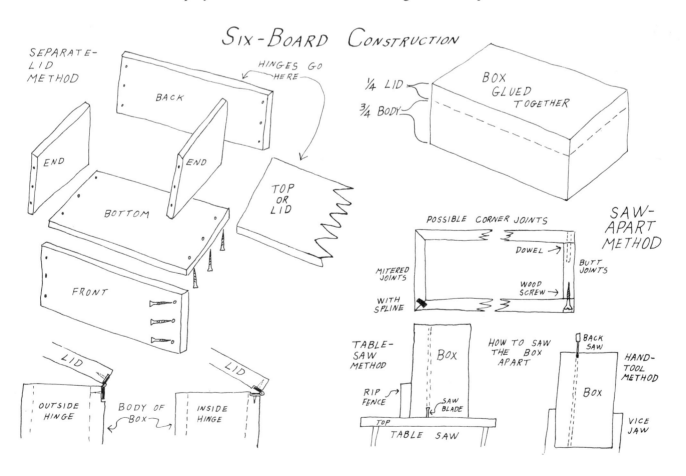

Box and the Northwest Coast Indian Box. The former is greatly appreciated in Europe especially in its round form, while the latter is one of the most unusual projects in the entire book.

Other boxes dealt with here are made principally by gluing up stock, like the square Salt & Pepper Shakers, or by drilling, which is used on the Stamp Caddy. The lathe is brought into play to create the Turned Boxes. The Birch-Bark Boxes employ both traditional American Indian construction methods and some modern techniques.

Decorating Boxes

Two of the most obvious ways to decorate the projects given here are carving and painting. These are shown on the Blanket Chest and the Indian Boxes. Another method is to cover the project with leather and decorate it with upholstering tacks. This technique is demonstrated on the Pioneer Trunk and the Briefcase. An appliqué approach is used on one of the Birch-Bark Boxes.

Another approach is to fasten things to a box. This is usually done on the lid and might include mineral specimens, seashells, fragments of precious stones, coral, etc. Wood, antler, and some of the above-mentioned items can also serve as handles on box lids. The circular, Birch-Bark Box has an unusual oak branch for a handle.

Inlaying items into box lids is yet another method of decoration. Some possibilities are coins, postage stamps, small lapidary pieces, and ceramic tiles, as used on the Bread Box project. One of my favorite methods of decorating box lids is with cutout sheet-metal inlays. Copper,

brass, and aluminum are inexpensive and easy to work and are splendid for this purpose. Sterling silver is easy to work but more expensive; nevertheless, it's a wonderful way to craft an heirloom.

Two examples of metal inlays are shown in the photo. The box on the left had a band-sawn body with wood of a contrasting color used for top and bottom. The top has an inlay of two sterling-silver initials. This was done by working up a template for the two letters and tracing around them onto 18-gauge silver. Next, the letters were cut out with a jeweler's saw and the edges dressed with needle files. Then, deciding on the placement of the initials on the cocobolo top, I carefully traced around them with a sharp-pointed art knife. The removal of the wood from inside these lines must

Boxes with metal inlays in the lids.

be done most gingerly with sharp, tiny tools. If your eyes are not up to this sort of fine work I suggest you employ some sort of magnifying setup. When the letters fitted snugly and flush with the lid, I glued them in with epoxy. To hold them in place while the epoxy set I clamped a board covered with wax paper to the lid. Later I smoothed the cocobolo lid with 600-grit paper and finally with crocus cloth. The box was finished with Danish oil and paste wax.

The box on the right was constructed using the six-board method and covered with leather. The logo was sawn out of sheet aluminum, as described above, and inlaid into the leather-covered lid. This is a much simpler approach than inlaying in wood and, even though this box is thirty years old, it's still functional and retains much of its original visual impact.

Sterling silver initials ready to be epoxied into cocobolo lid for a Band-Saw Box.

HARDWARE

The matter of hardware is much more important in box construction than it is with bowls, buckets, and baskets. Although some of the projects in this chapter require no hardware and a few get by with just hinges and/or handles, quite a few use hasps, corner braces, escutcheon plates and nails, or rivets with large fancy heads.

The obvious source of hardware is your local store and I have used commercial items on several projects. But what if your custom-made box cries out for something unusual? Most larger cities have at least one hardware store that carries a larger collection of items needed by the box-builder. Track these outlets down by using your local Yellow Pages and visit their premises. If they don't stock what you need, perhaps they will order it for you. Look also at the advertisements in woodworking magazines for mail-order outlets that specialize in distinctive hardware. Another possibility is to haunt flea markets, yard sales, and the like with a weathered eye for the perfect hasp or handles for the chest you are crafting. Keep in mind that it may be profitable to purchase

an old trunk just so you can cannibalize its hardware. If all these suggestions fail, consider having a local metalworker or blacksmith custom-make the items you need.

Still another way to acquire distinctive hardware is to make it yourself. I can hear some readers yelling foul at this statement. They will ask, how can a book that basically deals with woodworking dare to suggest that we try our hand at metalwork? Well, I do it with my head held high, because I believe it's both fun and rewarding to learn new skills and that no one is too old to tackle a different craft. I learned blacksmithing to earn a Boy Scout merit badge and have enjoyed pounding steel ever since.

Metalworking

If you decide to get involved in metalwork you can follow two rather distinct paths. The first is by far the easiest, in that it requires the fewest tools and the least commitment. I'll call this thin-metal blacksmithing. Don't think of this as second-class metalwork, because most of the fancy doors with showy strap hinges that I have observed around the world on commercial build-

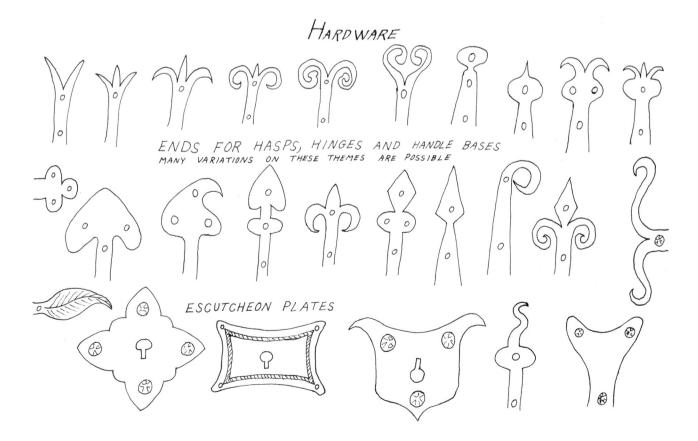

HARDWARE

ENDS FOR HASPS, HINGES AND HANDLE BASES
MANY VARIATIONS ON THESE THEMES ARE POSSIBLE

ESCUTCHEON PLATES

ings, churches, and homes employ this method. For small- to medium-size boxes, mild steel plate ⅛ inch thick and rods or bars of ¼ to ⅜ inch size will do nicely. Brass and copper can also be used. Metal of this sort can be cut with hack or sabre saw and smoothed with files or a bench grinder. Some bends can be made cold but for others you will need a torch, camp stove, or charcoal fire. Ball and crosspeen hammers can be used to bend the steel over a piece of railroad track or the anvil on a machinist's vise. These same hammers can be used to decorate the face of the items you make. This sort of metalwork is not illegal, immoral, or fattening, so give it a try and you will be amazed at the hinges and hasps you can turn out. These techniques can also be used to change the shapes and peen the surfaces of commercial hardware. The drawing on the previous page shows some hardware ideas for thin-metal blacksmithing.

Setting Up a Forge

Of course, if you really want to jump into metalworking with both feet you will need a forge. A very serviceable one can be made by following the plans in this chapter. I have made several of these and provided the forced draft with vacuum-cleaner or bathroom exhaust fans. I even tried a hair-dryer fan once but it was underpowered. A chunk of railroad track will do for a pounding surface but eventually you will want a real anvil, even if only a small one. You will also need at least one pair of tongs. To find these check your Yellow Pages under farrier supplies or visit junk yards and farm auctions. With this basic setup you will be able to manufacture most of the hardware you will need. Some possibilities are shown in the drawing. I do suggest that you read a book on blacksmithing before you get started, so you won't have to learn too many things by trial and error.

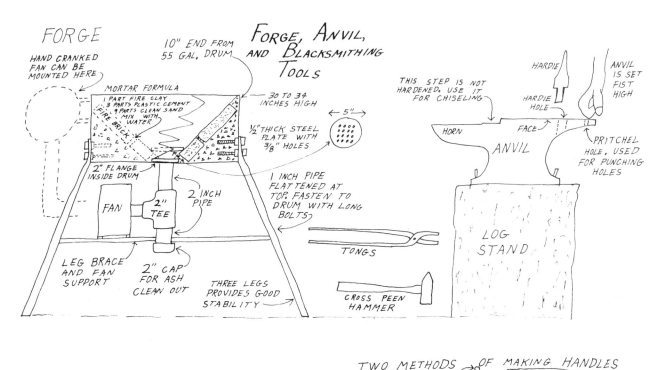

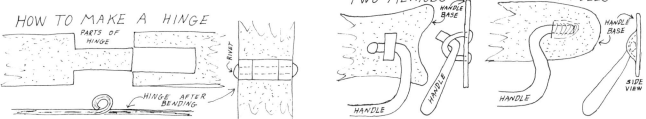

WOODS

Some of these projects depend on attractive woods to look their best; for others almost any wood will do. I will name the woods used if they have a bearing on construction or finish. A few of the boxes use a number of woods and I'll usually refer to these as mixed hardwoods.

A high percentage of the wood used was recycled from pallets, mill ends, or lumber destined to be burned. Often the size of a box was determined by the length and width of boards I had on hand. I never allowed my planned proportions to be altered but I did make boxes larger or smaller to fit my inventory. In the Bentwood Boxes qualities of flexibility are demanded and with a few of the novelty boxes I searched for woods with a weathered look. To me, finding suitable wood for projects is part of the fun of craftwork. Good hunting and great boxmaking!

PROJECTS

Basic Box

This is about as basic as a box can be made. I used six-board construction with mitred corners and a rabbeted top and bottom. The only hardware used were a piano hinge and a small brass hasp with a built-in hook. Oak and red lauan were the major woods utilized. Yellow glue was used for all joints, although I would recommend adding wood screws for strength if you make a larger

size. I made all cuts and sanded the inside surfaces first. Then I glued the six panels together being careful not to use an excess of glue that would drip inside the box.

When the glue was dry I sanded the outside and sawed the box apart. This can be done by making four passes over a table saw or by hand with a backsaw. The proportion I like is to allow about one-quarter of the height of the box for the lid and three-quarters for the body. The final jobs were making a tray, attaching the hardware and applying two coats of polyurethane.

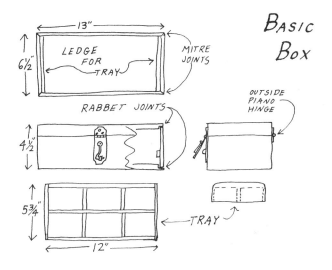

Basic Box being cut apart with a backsaw.

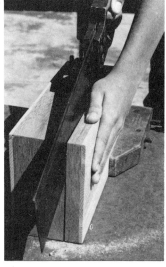

It's a basic box, for sure, but its uses are legion. In this size it can be used for jewelry, hobby supplies, collections, correspondence or silverware. A larger version could hold tools or toys.

Basic Box showing full tray.

Strongbox

I grew up in a small town where the Saturday-night double feature was the favorite activity of most lads, if we could earn the dime for admission. One of the pictures was always a Western and quite often it involved a stagecoach robbery. After the stage was halted a gravelly-voiced bad guy would invariably yell to the driver, "Throw down that strongbox." The scene was full of high drama and it made a big impression on me. No, I didn't want to rob stagecoaches, I wanted to make strongboxes.

My first Strongbox was made many years ago and it was a labor of necessity. We were going to host a fund-raising activity for a nonprofit organization and the volunteer cashier wanted a box that could be locked. I made a box of hard maple and oak and reinforced it with steel rods in the top and bottom and long screws in the sides. The hinges were factory-made but I forged the hasp and handles. It had slots for coins and bills in a tray and room beneath that for checks. All in all it was quite functional, but I thought it lacked elegance and needed more ironwork.

I have made a number of Strongboxes since that first one. Two are pictured here. The larger is made of ash and has a copious amount of forge work. To me this one comes closest to being the strongbox of the Western movies of yesteryear.

Strongbox with hardware.

The handmade nails do hold all of the hardware in place but they are not riveted over on the inside but rather are set in holes with epoxy. The ash consists of mill ends from a cabinet shop and the steel is recycled from broken fence posts. It weighs in at 52 pounds. This box, perhaps more than any other in this chapter, has a certain rugged primitiveness about it and this seems in keeping with its historic predecessors.

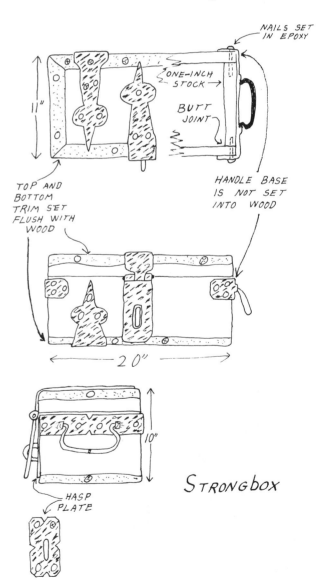

NAILS SET IN EPOXY

ONE-INCH STOCK

BUTT JOINT

11"

TOP AND BOTTOM TRIM SET FLUSH WITH WOOD

HANDLE BASE IS NOT SET INTO WOOD

20"

10"

HASP PLATE

STRONGBOX

The slightly smaller chest is of oak with mitred cuts on all edges, even the top and bottom. It has less ironwork, but what there is is considerably

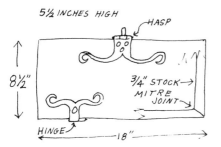

Smaller oak strongbox from back.

more delicate than on the first box. Here again the showy nails are set in epoxy. This box is a comparative lightweight at 13 pounds. In our home these two boxes function as plant holders, for storage, and as conversation pieces.

Tool Box

When I was a boy all the carpenters I knew carried their tools in a box like this. With these hand

tools they could build an entire house including framing, siding, roofing, lathing, and interior trim. As power tools became available, some carpenters adapted their boxes to hold them while others kept their hand tools in such a box but carried their power tools separately.

There was a simplistic beauty in these rugged boxes. The length was determined by the length of the two or three hand saws they carried. The remainder of the box had to be wide enough to hold a brace, hammer, square, etc. The drill bits and chisels were carried in canvas rolls. Holes were drilled inside to keep small tools, like nail sets, in place. Work out the dimensions for your box based on the hand and power tools you plan to carry.

Construction is basic and simple. First, cut all pieces to size, round the exposed edges, and sand all parts. Then fasten it together with wood screws and glue. Use strong wood and long screws to be sure of a sturdy box. I finished this box of mixed hardwood with three coats of spar urethane. This same box design can be used for other types of tools or gardening supplies.

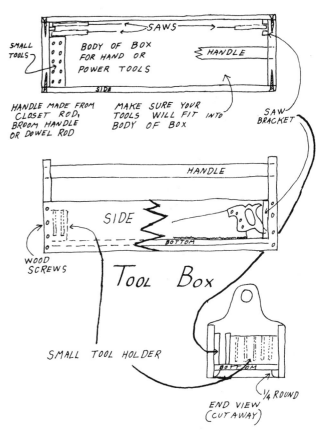

Bread Box

Bread Box with lid not assembled (*above*). Note cutting board and knife holder.

There was a time when all bread was unsliced and loaves were kept in a bread box. Then the bread-slicing machine was invented and most bread started to come sliced and wrapped, so many of the bread boxes became extinct. But I like to bake bread so I find a bread box very handy. What I always found unhandy was gathering the bread, and a cutting board, and a knife together in order to secure a slice of the staff of life. For that reason, this project has a breadboard and knife holder built right in.

The construction is basic. The diagonal lid is at a 45-degree angle and is hinged on two finishing nails driven in from the sides. I used mitred joints on the back but that was a matter of choice. The breadboard rides on two runners attached to the front and back. Mine will pull out in either direction but you can design your box so it pulls out in only one direction. I held this project together with yellow glue and finishing nails and applied one coat of salad bowl lacquer.

The diagonal lid is decorated with an old blue-and-white Dutch ceramic tile. The tile is set into the lid about ¼ inch and held in place with epoxy. This treatment is an easy and attractive way to decorate boxes with any pretty tile, or similar item you have gathering dust on a shelf.

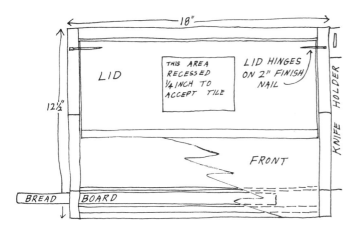

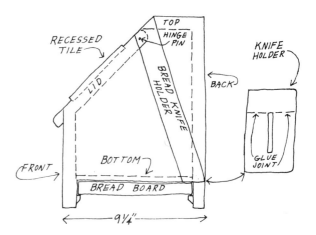

Lunch Box

On television, people usually eat lunch in fancy places but many Americans still carry a lunch box, and in my opinion many of these are poorly designed and out of touch with modern times. I built my first lunch box years ago and proceeded through many innovations to arrive at this design.

Newly completed Lunch Box open for inspection. An older one is shown from the back.

The standard lunch box of my youth contained a narrow-mouthed vacuum bottle that was positioned on its side and sometimes leaked. It had room for four to six sandwiches plus fruit and cookies. When people put in ten hours of really hard work, they might have needed that much food. Today,

the space allotted for our more high-energy foods is far too much. Rather, the space is needed to accommodate more fluids. The introduction of the wide-mouth thermos has even made it practical to carry hot stew or cold fruit salad. This box holds two such bottles, making for wide flexibility in meal planning.

I carried a box like this when I did botanic research work in the mountains where the only snacks available were a few wild berries. In cold weather, I packed hot tea in one thermos and stew or chili in the other, along with a sandwich and an apple. During the heat of summer, both bottles

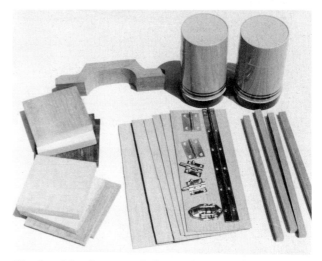

Wood and hardware needed to make a Lunch Box.

BILL OF MATERIALS

Number	Part Name	Size in Inches	Comments
4	Tops and bottoms	$4\frac{3}{4} \times 4\frac{3}{4} \times \frac{3}{4}$	Two pieces dished out for thermos
4	Shelves, top and bottom	$4\frac{3}{4} \times 4\frac{3}{4} \times \frac{3}{16}$	Two pieces cut out for top of thermos
4	Back brace	$\frac{1}{2} \times \frac{1}{2} \times 12$	Use any strong wood
4	Front brace	$\frac{1}{8} \times 2 \times 12$	Cut from same plywood used for sides
6	Sides and Backs	$\frac{1}{8} \times 5 \times 12$	Some edges require mitering
4	Finish top and bottom	$\frac{1}{4} \times 5 \times 5$	Dark wood used for contrast
1	handle	$1\frac{1}{2} \times 2\frac{1}{2} \times 10$	To be sawn into handle shape

Hardware

Number	Part Name	Size in Inches	Comments
1	Piano hinge	12 inches long	Fasten to side of box with wood screws
2	Small hinges		Fasten to shelf with wood screws and to back with small bolts
2	Barrel bolts		To hold shelves on top of thermos—barrel bolt goes into hole in front brace
1	Snap latch		Holds front of box closed

held liquids. I discovered that, when turned on its side, this box made a passable stool when the ground was damp.

The key to the dimensions of your box will be the size of the wide-mouth thermos you use. I have given the dimensions I used, but only as a point of reference. Cut the bottom pieces to fit your bottles and build everything else around these pieces. I used thin plywood for the sides and shelves and hardwood for the remainder. As this project is best assembled in a definite way, here are illustrated, step-by-step instructions:

1. Cut all pieces to size (see materials list) and sand smooth.
2. Dish out bottom pieces to hold thermos bottles.
3. Glue the two shelf pieces together.
4. Glue front and rear braces to the top and bottom.
5. Mitre the rear edge of sides and glue them in place.
6. Mitre both edges of back and glue in place.
7. Trim shelf to fit and drill holes for its hinge.
8. Trim the finished top and bottom to size and glue in place.
9. Fasten the two sections of the box together with the piano hinge.
10. Glue the handle to the top of the box. When the glue is set, saw the handle apart and reinforce with wood screws from the inside.
11. Affix barrel bolt and hinge to shelves and fasten shelves inside the lunch box.
12. Attach snap latch.
13. Finish box with two or more coats of spar urethane.

Partially assembled Lunch Box.

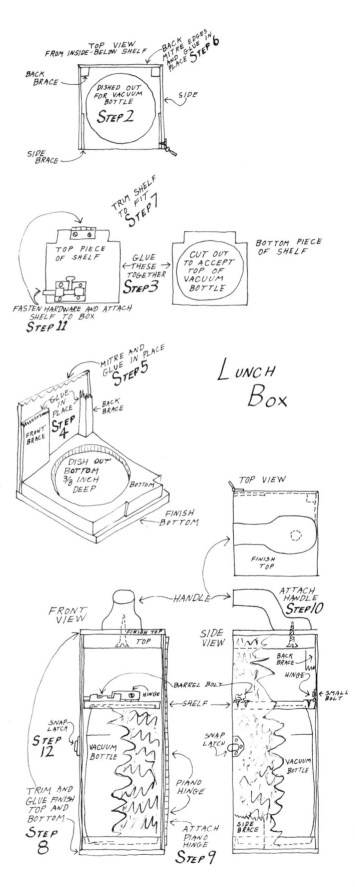

Hobby Chest

Having been overly hobby-oriented all of my life, I was thrilled to see the neat wooden chests, chuck full of drawers, that came on the market a few years back. However, I was not thrilled with the hefty prices and decided to build my own. I had just traded for some short pieces of Philippine mahogany 1 by 6 that I figured would be perfect for the carcass and I already had some thinner apitong on hand for the drawers. The basic chest is six-board construction with a ¼-inch plywood back and an open front. I held the carcass together with yellow glue and ¼-inch dowel pins. Your major decision is to decide on the number and size of the drawers. I keep tools and supplies for silversmithing, wood carving, and fly tying in my chest and this layout of four shallow half drawers, two deep half drawers, two shallow full drawers, and one deep full drawer has worked well for me. But you should analyze your needs and design your chest accordingly.

You can use any of the standard types of drawer hardware or use scrap aluminum for drawer glides as I did. I often use this system and find it easy to construct and flawless in operation. Both right-angle and channel aluminum can be used. My method is to mount it on the inside of the chest carcass and saw corresponding grooves on the drawer sides. The drawer pulls are a design

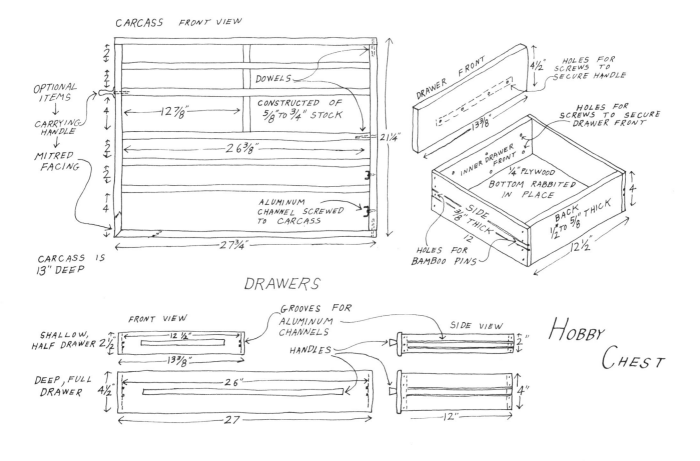

I like. You can grab them at any point and get the drawer open and they are a fine way to use up thin scrap. I always make them of contrasting wood for visual impact. The drawer handle and the two fronts are put together with wood screws and the sides are attached with $\frac{1}{16}$-inch bamboo pins. The mitred facing on the front of the chest is a bit wider than the lumber used in the carcass. Its purpose is to hide the aluminum drawer glides.

Hobby Chest with two drawers partially open.

Band-Saw Box

This is a clever way to make a wide variety of small boxes. Although I prefer the band saw, any good jigsaw can be used. The boxes can also be made by hand with a coping saw. The material can be driftwood, burl, chunks of root, edges of planks, glued-up stock, "mountain driftwood," or just ordinary pieces of wood. This is a fine project for putting odd-shaped pieces of wood to use.

Five completed Band-Saw Boxes. The top two are drift-wood with no finishing material applied.

The wood can be left in its natural state, sand-blasted, painted, carved, charred and wire-brushed, or sanded and finished with stain and/or varnish. Mountain driftwood is my name for chunks of weathered wood found in the high country. The rugged mountain weather can sculpture wood just like ocean waves.

Band-Saw Boxes under construction.

Once you have some suitable pieces of wood at hand you must decide where to make the cuts to turn your wood into a box. These cuts can be straight or curved but should be made with a sharp blade to produce as smooth a surface as possible. There are two slightly different ap-

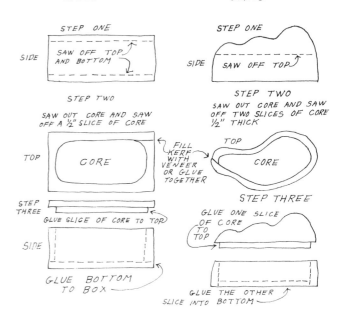

proaches to doing this but they give about the same results. The major difference is whether you want a glue joint on the side of the box or on the bottom.

The kerf made by the band saw when passing through the box to cut out the core can be filled with a piece of veneer or simply glued closed. Gluing the kerf closed is recommended for cutting method #2 so the tighter fit will hold the bottom in place. I often cover the inside of my Band-Saw Boxes with felt and the bottoms with sheet cork.

Table-Saw Box

Here is a really odd way to make a box from the short pieces of timber often found at construction sites. If you think about it, however, it is really quite a logical approach to making a container. Everyone uses table saws to make deep, wide grooves. This is simply an extension of this technology, as the entire body of the box is hollowed out with repeated passes over the saw blade.

A dado blade can be used for this but I usually make a series of cuts 1 inch deep and about ½ inch apart. I chisel out the waste and repeat the process until the box is as deep as I desire. I then remove the waste down to the bottom of the box as neatly as possible. I don't strive for perfection on this operation because I always cover the bottom and possibly the sides of these boxes with felt, cork, or similar material.

Next I fit the ends for the box. I usually employ rabbet joints for this, but many other systems could be used. As the body of these boxes is usually construction grade, I try to use some-

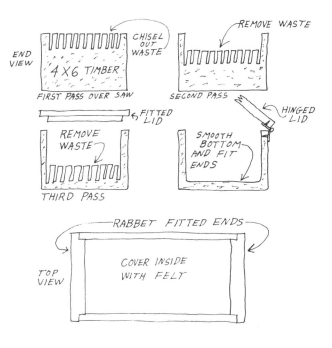

what fancier woods for the ends and top. The body of the two table-saw boxes shown here are both of Douglas fir and the ends are ash. The tops are of mixed hardwoods. The tops can be attached with piano hinges, as I did on both of these, or rabbeted to fit.

Utility Box

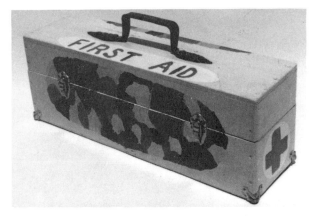

This was designed to hold a large first-aid kit which I carried in my vehicle for many years when I worked in the mountains. The shape lends itself for use as a fishing-tackle box, a depository for tools or hobby supplies, or for carrying small stuff needed during a trip. It is sturdily constructed of ⅜-inch plywood with solid 1-inch stock being used for the ends. It has brass corner

Utility Box

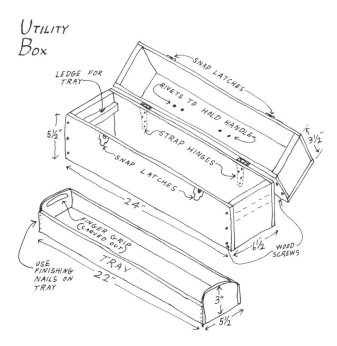

reinforcements on the bottom, strap hinges, a hand-forged handle and two snap latches for positive closing.

This Utility Box uses six-board construction with a high lid to accommodate a full tray. It is held together with flat-headed wood screws and yellow glue. If you plan to use your box in wet conditions I would recommend a fully waterproof glue. The box was given a coat of primer and then two coats of oil-based enamel. First-aid kits are usually rather drab affairs, but I wanted mine to be different. My children did the designs on the front and back when they were small. A bit primitive, but certainly colorful.

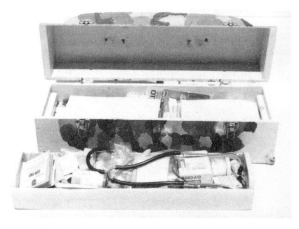

Opened Utility Box.

Novelty Boxes

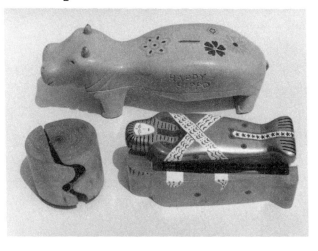

I use this title not for a specific type of box but rather to cover all the boxes that don't seem to fit into any other category. Three examples are shown here but the possibilities are just about endless—limited only by our imaginations. Just about any shaped piece of wood you come across can be converted into a container by removing material from the inside. All manner of carved animals, like the hippo shown here, are candidates for this treatment. Duck decoys are a prime example. Pyramids and other geometric shapes, like the turned cylinder in the photos, offer other possibilities. The mummy-shaped pencil box represents yet another type of novelty box.

The Happy Hippo bank was constructed from two scrap pieces of 4- by 6-inch Douglas fir. The profile was cut out on the bandsaw and the remaining shaping was handled with carving tools, spokeshave, and rasps. The body cavity that accepts the coins can be carved out or done with rotary burrs. As you can see in the drawing, this cavity is entirely in the top piece. The two parts of the hippo are held together with wood screws inserted from the bottom. I finished this novelty box bank with light blue paint and a few folk art flowers in red and yellow. For many years this box stood up to hard service as my son's depository for coins.

The cylindrical novelty box was fashioned from a short piece of olive wood log. The log was cut in two with a serpentine cut on the bandsaw using a narrow blade. The interior wood was drilled out and finished with a rotary tool. A 1/8-inch hole is drilled vertically through the serpentine cut and a dowel pin inserted, thus allowing the box to open

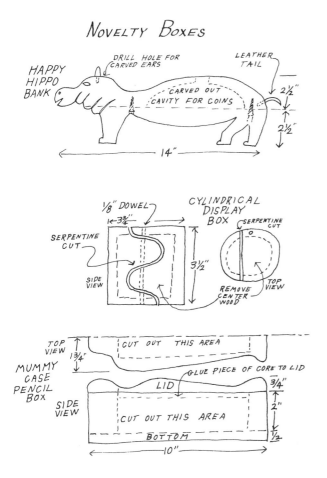

off and glued to the underside of the ¾-inch piece I planned to use for the lid to hold the lid in place. Next I glued a piece of ½-inch stock to the bottom. With the three pieces sandwiched together, I band-sawed out the outline of the mummy case. Then I carved the profile of the mummy case on the lid, sanded it smooth, and applied paint. Consult your local library for decorating ideas. I took some of my designs from mummy cases I saw in the Egyptian Museum in Cairo.

Drilled Box

This method of making a box is related to those used in fashioning the bandsaw box: the difference being that the waste wood is drilled out instead of being sawn out in a core. A 2- or 3-inch Forstner bit is ideal for this job but spade and brad bits can also be used.

In the example shown here a weathered piece of manzanita root was used. I first studied the piece to ascertain the best place to saw off the lid

and close. This box, which was designed to display geology specimens, was finished with paste wax. Other uses would be to show off prized fishing lures, toy soldiers, and the like.

I made the pencil box in the shape of a mummy case by scroll-sawing a rectangle, the length of the pencils I wanted to store, in a piece of 2-inch stock. A piece of this core was sawed

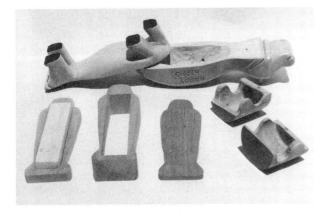

Three Novelty Boxes prior to assembly.

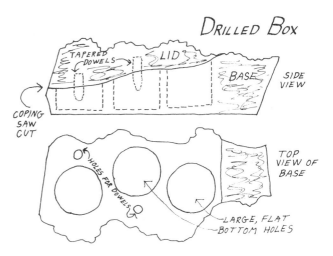

to show its interesting texture. I made this undulating cut with a coping saw for fear of hitting a rock if I used my bandsaw. Once the lid is removed it is just a matter of drilling one or more large holes in the base to hold jewelry, coins, pills, etc. The easiest way to hold the lid in place is by matching two or three ⅜-inch dowel pins in the lid with corresponding holes in the base. No finish was applied to this box.

If your shop is like mine you have probably acquired some nice pieces of burl, driftwood, or root. The drilled box is an easy way to turn these pieces into attractive containers, so get busy and reduce the clutter in your shop.

Salt & Pepper Shakers

There are many ways to make salt and pepper shakers. Here are two methods that consist essentially of making little boxes with a few small holes in the top and one large one in the bottom which can be plugged with a cork. Either method is a great way to use those tag ends of fine woods that seem to pile up in every active shop.

Parts of a vertical salt shaker of oak.

In the vertical method a series of "U"-shaped pieces are glued between two solid pieces of wood. The open end of the "U", which is the bottom of the shaker, is sealed with a ½-inch piece with a cork-sized hole in it. This piece is positioned so that the cork will protrude enough for easy removal. I do the entire glue job in one clamping and then plane and sand the shakers smooth. Next I drill the shaker holes in the top using ³⁄₃₂-inch bits for large shakers and ¹⁄₁₆-inch bits for small models.

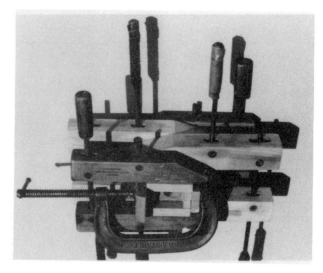

A vertical salt shaker being glued.

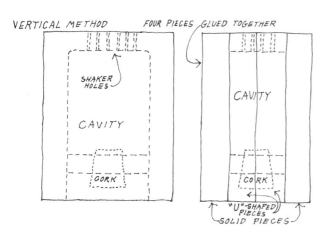

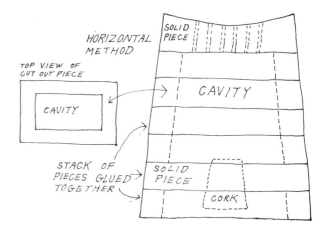

Pieces needed to make horizontal-type salt and pepper shakers.

The horizontal method involves the stacking and gluing of pieces of wood. The top piece and the one next to the bottom are solid while all of the others are sawed or drilled out. The top piece is drilled with shaker holes and the piece next to the bottom is drilled for the cork.

A black walnut horizontal pepper shaker being sanded.

Either of these methods can be used to make shakers that are square, rectangular, or octagonal, with tapered or straight sides, or with flat, concave, or convex tops. The examples shown here are large, for use at a barbecue, but they can be made smaller for table use.

I use several marking schemes to differentiate salt and pepper shakers. One of the simplest is to make the salt shakers from light-colored woods like maple, birch, beech, ash, or oak and the pepper shakers from black walnut or mahogany. Another easy way is to drill the shaker holes in the shape of an "S" or "P". Still another way is to fashion the shakers with somewhat different shapes, such as a concave top for salt and a convex top for pepper. And, of course, you can identify the contents with an "S" or a "P" on the side or spell out SALT and PEPPER. A variation on this is to use another language to designate the contents; for example, salt is *salz* in German, *zalts* in Yiddish, *sal* in Spanish, *sel* in French, *zout* in Dutch and *sale* in Italian, while pepper is *pfeffer* in German, *peppar* in Swedish, *pimienta* in Spanish and *poivre* in French.

My way of marking the shakers is to outline or carve out the letters with a round, carbide-tipped rotary burr and then to burn the area with an electric pencil. I usually finish my shakers with brushing lacquer or Danish oil, being careful not to get finishing material inside the shaker.

Bentwood Box

This is the first of many projects in this book involving the bending of wood. If you failed to read the technical notes on this subject in the introductory chapter I recommend that you do so now.

Bentwood Box is a radical departure from the six-board construction that was employed for the earlier projects in this chapter. Only four pieces of wood are used to make these boxes but two of these are bent. This is what I call light-duty bending, so a steam box is not required. These boxes can be made oval, round, or pear-shaped and can be crafted in small sizes for jewelry or larger for craft supplies, cookies, or as presentation boxes for homemade cheese.

I'll start by telling you how I make oval boxes like those shown in the photos and then explain some of the variations. My first action is to bandsaw out two bottoms from ⅜- or ½-inch stock and trim these to size on a disk sander. I also sand the top and bottom surfaces of these pieces before proceeding. Next I saw some pieces of ash ⅟₁₆ to ³⁄₃₂ inch thick from a full 2-inch board using a

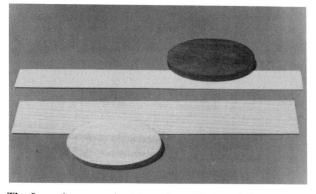

The four pieces required to make a Bentwood Box.

thin kerf, carbide-tipped blade on my table saw. These are hand-scraped to remove any saw marks. I cut these pieces to length figuring on a 2-inch overlap. These thin pieces are clamped to the edge of a 2 by 6 and tapered on opposite sides with a block plane so they will match nicely when overlapped.

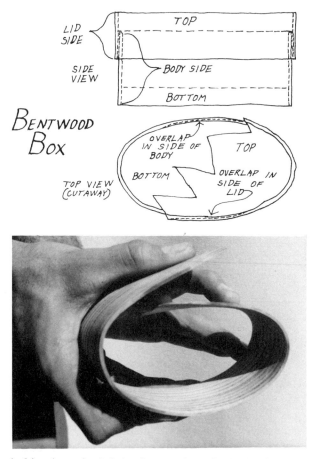

A thin piece of ash being bent to form the body of a Bentwood Box.

The piece to be bent can be soaked in a sink or large pan. I start with hot water and soak the piece for 12 hours. Then, before bending, I give the piece two soaks of one hour each in very hot water. Wrapping the thin piece around the bottom, I hold it in place with cord or heavy rubber bands. I insert the other bottom piece in the open end to help the box keep its shape while drying for 24 hours. Then I apply yellow glue to the edge of the bottom and to the overlap and tie the thin side tight again. I cover the bottom piece, used as a spacer, with plastic wrap during this operation so it won't get glued into place.

A Bentwood Box body being glued. Heavy rubber bands are used as clamps.

Next I use the body of the box to figure the size of the lid. This can easily be done by tracing around the body on the stock to be used for the top. I often use fancier woods for the top, like co-cobolo. The bending of the thin side piece for the lid is done exactly as it was for the body of the box. For these boxes I used ⅟₁₆-inch American holly, 1¼ inches wide. When the lid is completed I finish-sand my Bentwood Box, ending with 600-grit paper, and then apply polyurethane varnish or Danish oil.

Bentwood Boxes larger than 8 inches in diameter should have sides around ⅛ inch thick and somewhat thicker tops and bottoms. In Switzerland, larger-size boxes are sometimes laced with rattan where they overlap. Leather thongs could also be used. In Scandinavia, as well as Central Europe, these boxes are often decorated with colorful tole painting. Another way to make these boxes colorful is to glue up pieces of contrasting woods for the tops. Also consider adding turned or carved handles to the lids.

Indian Box

I plead guilty of overworking the word "unique," but I feel it is the only word that does justice to this unusual container. The Northwest Coast Indians, who devised this three-piece box, lived in a benevolent climate where the plentiful salmon kept them well fed and where some of the choicest timber trees of North America grew in their backyards. With time on their hands, marvelous material for the taking, and inventive minds, they gave us decorated plank houses, Chilkat blankets, totem poles, and this version of the bentwood box. Considering that they were a small gathering of tribes, they made a tremendous contribution to the world of arts and crafts.

I had read about these boxes as a lad but first saw them at the Alaska State Museum in 1953 when I was in that state on an expedition studying glaciers. What creativity it took to come up with a box that uses one plank for all four sides. What fine craftsmanship was involved in making these boxes so watertight that they could be used for cooking by adding hot rocks to the contents. These boxes were also used for storing food and clothing. The Tlingit, Haida, Tsimshian, Bella Coola, Kwakiutl, Nootka, and Coast Salish used

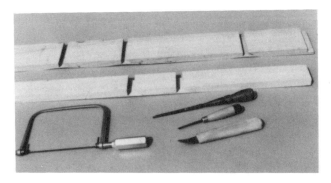

Notched pieces for Indian Boxes.

red or yellow western cedar for their boxes but you can use any straight-grained, quarter-sawn, flawless wood that is suitable for bending.

The thing that allows the sides to be made from one plank are three grooves that are cut about seven-eighths of the way through the wood. The remaining thin piece of wood becomes the hinge that allows the plank to bend and thus form the four sides. In my sketch I show one of the old ways of grooving a plank, a modern way that is sometimes used on commercial boxes, and the way used by most custom box-makers today. You will note that the last system provides the longest hinge and thus offers the greatest likelihood of success. It is the only system I use. However, this is one project where you may well have some failures before crafting a suitable piece.

Figuring out the dimensions for this sort of box can be a bit tricky. I have included some figures for a small box, but the dimensions of the finished box will depend on how thick your wood hinge is and also its degree of flexibility. My rule of thumb is to make my grooves as wide as they are deep, so if I am using stock a full inch thick both of these will be ⅞ inch. The fourth corner of the box is put together with a rabbet joint. When the box is glued together this joint can be sanded round to match the bent joints.

To make an Indian Box, first lay out the wood for the sides and cut the three grooves and the rabbet joint. I find the most valuable tools for this

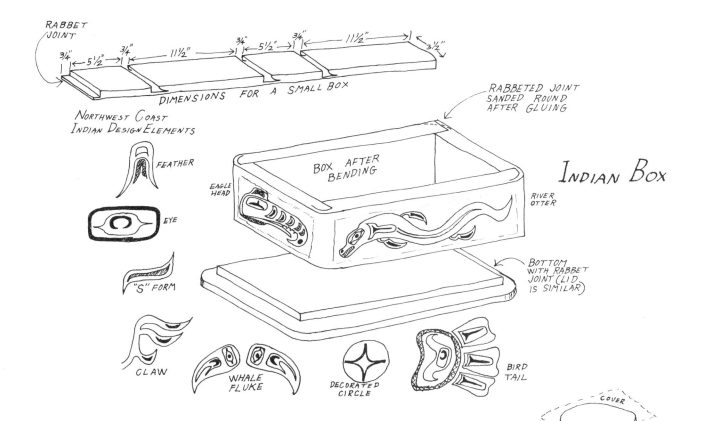

RABBET JOINT

3/4" | 5 1/2" | 3/4" | 11 1/2" | 3/4" | 5 1/2" | 3/4" | 11 1/2" | 3 1/2"

DIMENSIONS FOR A SMALL BOX

NORTHWEST COAST INDIAN DESIGN ELEMENTS

FEATHER

EYE

"S" FORM

CLAW

WHALE FLUKE

DECORATED CIRCLE

BIRD TAIL

RABBETED JOINT SANDED ROUND AFTER GLUING

BOX AFTER BENDING

EAGLE HEAD

RIVER OTTER

INDIAN BOX

BOTTOM WITH RABBET JOINT (LID IS SIMILAR)

job are band and back saws, chisels, a crooked knife, and rasps. Strive to make these grooves uniform and accurate so that each bend will be alike. Heavy-duty steaming is required to form this box, so a few hours in a steam box is the ideal treatment for preparing the wood. Lacking a steam box I started by soaking the wood in a bathtub in hot water for 48 hours. Next I built a fire under a clean 55-gallon drum that contained four inches of water and some bricks to keep the wood above the water level.

I placed my pieces of ash, white oak, and holly in the drum, laid a metal cover over the opening, and steamed the wood for a full hour. The wood was then flexible and I bent each piece into a rectangle and applied clamps. It is really quite a thrill when a straight plank turns into the sides of a box before your eyes. After allowing the wood to dry for two days I fitted a rabbeted bottom to each box and glued this in place at the same time that I glued the four corner joints.

At this point it's important to check that the rim of the box is square and level. If it is, make a rabbeted top that fits the box and sand everything smooth. The Indian box-makers seemed to abhor

COVER

WOOD

BRICKS

WATER

ROCK

FIRE

ROCK

My makeshift steaming rig for Indian Boxes.

A steamed piece of an Indian Box after bending and clamping.

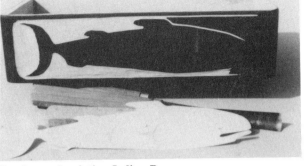

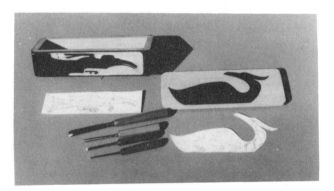

Carving and painting Indian Boxes.

any open spaces and endeavored to cover every square inch of their creations with the stylized animals for which their art is known. I take a different approach and select only a few choice motifs to decorate my boxes.

There are examples of Northwest Coast Indian designs in many books on Indian art so you should have no trouble finding material at your library. I always alter the designs I find to give them a personal touch. Colors used in the authentic designs are red, black, and occasionally a bit of blue-green. These three colors, along with the natural-wood background, might seem a bit limiting but you will find they are adequate to do the job.

The simplest way to decorate an Indian Box is to just paint the design on with oil-base enamel. I prefer to do relief carving first, to make the design stand out, then proceed with the painting. Another favorite way to decorate Indian Boxes is to paint the various sides either red or black. Then, when the paint is dry, I do the relief carving. By carving through the painted surface I can achieve sharper lines and greater detail than using even the tiniest brush. Of course, other colors can be added to the surfaces after carving. These last two methods are used on the three boxes shown in the photos. Finally, I give my boxes a coat of polyurethane.

All three of the boxes pictured were designed to hold jewelry. The white-oak box features mammals in its decoration, the one of ash wood shows birds, and the box fashioned of holly carries fish and sea denizen motifs. In larger sizes these could serve as toy boxes, blanket chests, or gen-

eral storage receptacles. A really unusual coffee table could be made from an Indian Box 17 inches high covered with a piece of thick glass overhanging all sides. Indian Boxes are probably the most difficult project in this book to complete in that they demand a wide-ranging group of skills. These skills go beyond accurate cutting and fitting and bring into play a combination of woodworking judgment and hand–eye coordination. I wish you luck in mastering this technique. Be thankful you don't have to do your bending on the beach using seaweed and hot rocks as the Northwest Coast Indians did.

Shadow Box

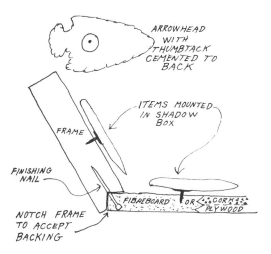

If my memory serves me accurately shadow boxes were quite popular when I was a boy. Perhaps that makes them old-fashioned, but I find them a fine way to display a collection or to show off a few special pieces that you have made or found. This box is a one-evening table-saw project. Wood in sizes from 1 by 3 to 2 by 8 can be used for the frames, which can be made square or rectangular. I make the backing for my boxes from either fibre-board or ¼-inch plywood covered with ¼-inch sheet cork to facilitate mounting with thumbtacks, but more on that later.

To make this Shadow Box I set my table saw's mitre gauge to 63½ degrees and tilt the blade to 37¾ degrees. This gives the sides a steep enough rake to make them interesting but not so great an angle that they can't be used to mount display

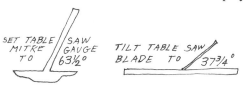

items. Then I saw one end of each of the frame pieces. Next I reverse the pieces and, using the same settings, cut the four pieces to length. I notch out each of the frame pieces at this time to accept the backing. The four box pieces are now glued together. I use finishing nails to add strength to larger-size boxes. The backing can now be nailed in place. Finishing is a matter of personal choice.

Display items can be mounted in a shadow box in many ways. I prefer to mount small things by

attaching thumbtacks to the backs of each item with contact cement. Then, to mount the arrowheads, knives, coins, medals, and so on, in the shadow box, I simply push the point of the tack into the backing material. With this system, it is easy to rearrange a display or to change it entirely. I should, however, warn you here not to fasten thumbtacks to any porous material with contact cement unless you plan to mount the item permanently.

Pocketknife ready for mounting in Shadow Box.

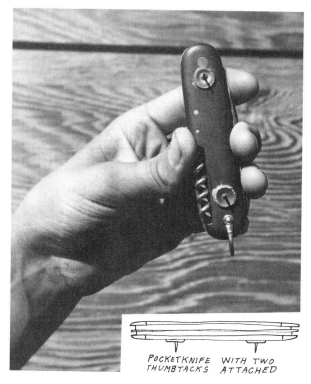

Skittles Box

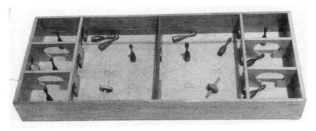

Here is an old tabletop game that offers action and surprises to competitors of any age. Any number can play and it makes no more noise than a game of billiards. I took the dimensions of this project from a skittles box I enjoyed playing with many years ago.

You can put the box together any way you like, but I used yellow glue on all joints along with ¼-inch dowels on the corners and finishing nails on the partitions. I also nailed through the ½-inch plywood base into the sides and partitions. The sides and partitions were made from mixed woods ⅜ to ⅝ inch thick. The pins are a simple between-centers lathe project. If you don't have a lathe you could carve suitable pins or simply use 4-inch lengths of ¾-inch dowel. You will need twelve pins but I suggest you turn thirteen in case one is lost. A homemade top can be turned or fashioned by inserting a 3½-inch piece of ¼-inch dowel through a hole in a 2-inch disk of wood. Both methods are shown in the illustration. Two coats of a tough polyurethane varnish are a good finish for this project.

Skittles can be played by individuals, or by two or more in teams. Score is kept by counting up the numbers of pins that are knocked over by the top. Each player wraps all or part of a 3-foot cord around the shaft of the top, and places the shaft in the groove at the end of the box, then passes the cord through the hole. Holding the top loosely in place with one hand, the player pulls the cord with the other. This launches the top on what is hoped will be a walk around the skittles box resulting in a high score.

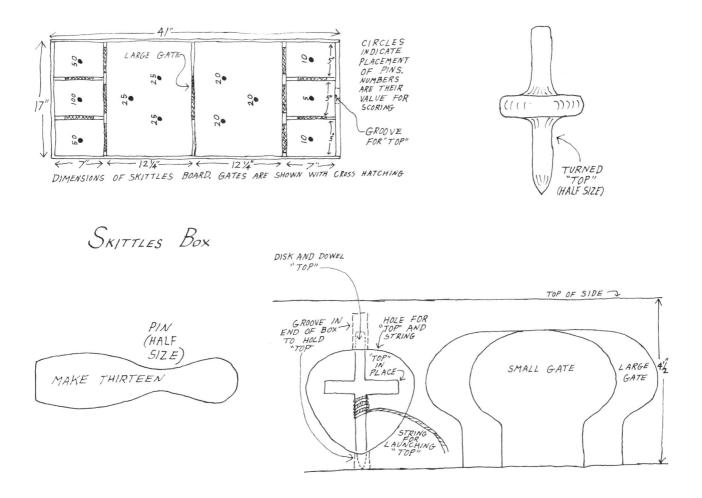

Labyrinth Boxes

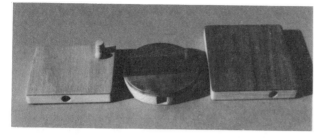

Most boxes are designed to be utilitarian or decorative, but here is another box that is just pure fun. It's the sort of game you place on your coffee table and let everyone have a chance, or you break it out at a party and challenge players to "beat the time." The object is to insert a marble on one side of the box and pass it through the maze by tilting the box until the marble appears at the other side. This is an easy project but you must be clever, perhaps even a bit diabolical, to outwit the players. I make my labyrinth boxes from shop scrap, but I sometimes use fancy woods for the top surface to end up with both an attractive box and a challenging game.

The size and shape of Labyrinth Boxes are up for grabs. I see no reason why they couldn't be made oval or octagonal but I have confined mine to round, square, and rectangular. Sizewise, I think that anything from six inches to a foot is perfectly fine.

I have used two rather distinct approaches in constructing these game boxes. In the first, the sides and the inner labyrinth walls are made from stock measuring ¼ by ¾ inches. The second method, that I used on the round box in the photo, involves sawing the circumference and the maze partitions from a solid piece of ¾-inch wood. Be sure you make two holes about ⅝ inch in diameter on opposite sides of the box for the passage in and out of the marble.

Doing the gluing in two stages works best for me. In the first gluing I attach the sides and maze walls to the base, which is usually a ⅛- or ¼-inch piece of plywood with nice veneer on one side. At this point I check the layout to be sure a marble will pass through all the passageways. If it does, I clamp the piece and let the glue dry. Next, I glue on the top, round the corners and edges, sand the project ending with 600-grit paper, and apply carnauba furniture wax.

The trick in making a challenging Labyrinth Box is to work in lots of traps and tricky turns that will impede the marble on its passage from hole to hole. Two layouts are shown in the drawing but I'm sure you can come up with others that are fiendishly conceived to drive your friends up the wall. One final reminder: Keep a plan of your Labyrinth Box so you will never forget just how the maze is laid out. It will help ensure that you will be able to beat anyone's time.

A completed Labyrinth Box and two without lids.

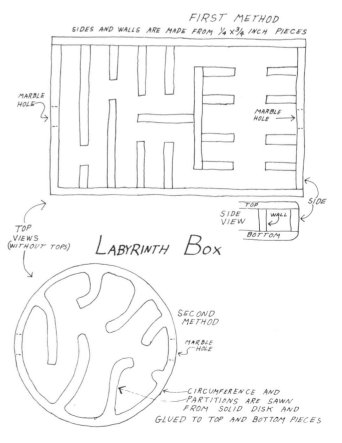

Block Boxes

When I was a lad, my favorite gifts were building blocks. I imagine I had most of the sizes and shapes then available, but I always welcomed another set. The colored blocks in the photo were one of these sets. When my son was small I decided to pass this set along to him but the original cardboard box had disintegrated and one block was lost. It was no problem for me to make a replacement block and, while at it, I made the beechwood box to put the set in. Later, when I designed a set of blocks for our three children, I also built a storage box to go with it.

Two boxes to hold children's blocks and a rod-block creation.

This handmade set of blocks, which we call rod-blocks, became a preferred rainy-day activity for our three youngsters and their friends. The primary pieces are ½-inch birch dowels and maple blocks 2, 4, 11, and 14 inches long. The two longer lengths have a larger hole near each end that allows the rods to turn and function as axles. The set also includes wheels and a few other pieces.

The box that holds all these pieces is made of pine and measures 6 by 8½ by 20. It has a sliding top, wheels, and a pull cord, so it functions as a pull toy as well as a receptacle for the rod-blocks.

This project is not a specific box design but rather a suggestion to all woodworking fathers, mothers, grandparents, etc., to make a sturdy container for their children's blocks. It will prevent the loss of the pieces and will help the youngsters keep their rooms in order. Naturally, you can also design a set of building blocks to go in the box.

Briefcase

There are handsome wooden briefcases on the market but when I decided to make one I made no attempt to imitate these styles. Rather, I analyzed my needs and designed my case to fill those specific needs. I decided I needed a strong container of average size with hard flat sides that could be used as a lap desk when flying. The result was a drawer-type, leather-covered briefcase that serves my needs admirably.

The outside measurements of the case are 3½ by 13¼ by 16 inches. It is constructed of ⅜-inch plywood with ½-inch solid wood ends. It is put together with yellow glue and countersunk, flathead wood screws. On the inside, the drawer measures 2⅜ by 12 by 14. The drawer sides were fashioned from 5⁄16-inch Philippine mahogany and the bottom from rosewood veneer plywood. Fin-

Briefcase with drawer partly extended.

ishing nails and yellow glue were used on the joints and the exposed mahogany was finished with polyurethane.

The leather cover gives my briefcase the look of an expensive piece of luggage. It also forms the handles and provides a nice working surface when the case is used as a lap desk. I used a tan, lightweight cowhide for the covering, with brown, pebble-grained calfskin for the handle and tab reinforcements. If you don't like this two-tone effect, you can, of course, use only one type of leather. Another option would be to make only the handles and closing tabs of leather and allow the wood to show on all the other surfaces.

The drawing shows how the one-piece leather cover is cut. I hand-stitched the handle reinforcements onto this piece and then glued it to the case with contact cement. Unless you are very experienced at cementing leather to wood you may elect to attach only the bottom and the two large sides

at first. The final fitting on the two narrow ends can then be done, after which they are cemented in place. I used brass upholstering tacks to form a pattern on these narrow end pieces. These tacks also secure the leather closing tabs. Note that before these tabs are hand-stitched the female portion of a leather snap is fastened to the cowhide.

A piece of cowhide is wrapped around the outside of the drawer with the seam at the back of the drawer. Before this piece is put in place with contact cement, a reinforced leather drawer pull is stitched to it. Also the male portion of the two leather snaps are fastened to the cowhide to engage the snaps on the tabs. I burned my initials onto one side of the case. I use this "brand" to tell me when the drawer is right side up. This briefcase has served me well for many years. Its only upkeep has been an occasional rubdown with carnauba leather cream.

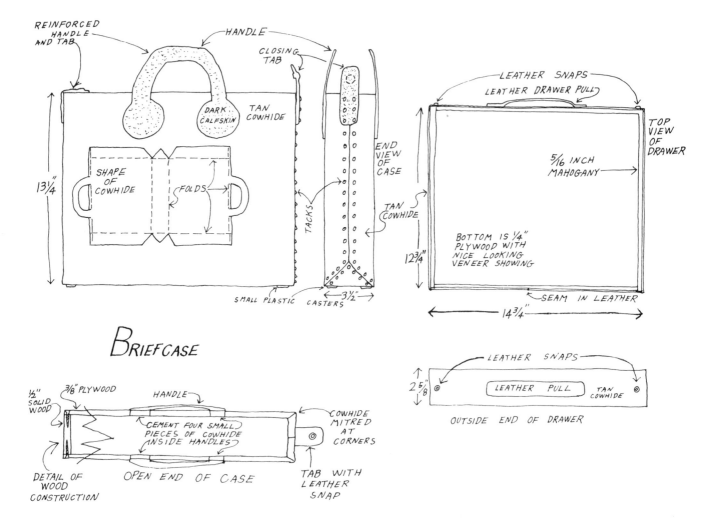

Turned Boxes

I wonder if anyone knows when the first turned box was made. I have never heard a date mentioned but I suspect it was shortly after the invention of the lathe, and that was a long time ago. Turned boxes are, of course, round. Notwithstanding that similarity, they can take on many forms.

In size they can vary from tiny jewelry boxes, to medium-sized herb containers, to large cookie jars. The lids can be left plain, inlaid with metal, bone, or contrasting woods, or include a turned handle or one affixed later. The sides of the body of a turned box can be decorated on the lathe, or by carving or painting when the turning is completed. The bodies of the two small, straight-sided boxes in the photo were left natural, that is, not turned on the outside. If the bark had been tight, I would have allowed it to remain on the boxes. The few examples shown here are meant solely to stimulate your creative thinking because the possibilities are just about endless.

I always turn the body of the box first. This is faceplate turning, but I often run the tail stop up and allow the dead center to help stabilize the work. Forming the outside of the box is basic lathe work where both cutting and scraping techniques can be utilized. For removing waste from the inside of the box I prefer round-nosed and diamond-point tools. When the body is completed

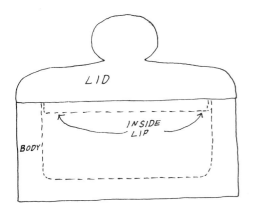

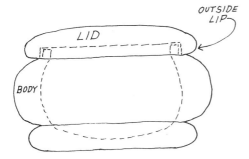

Turned Box and lid still mounted on lathe faceplate. The chisel blade indicates where the turning will be pried loose from the mounting block.

I turn the lid also, mounted on a faceplate. Measurements are more critical on the lid because you want it to fit snugly on the body. The drawing shows two ways of making a lid. I call these the inside and outside lip methods. They are equally satisfactory but I would judge method one to be the strongest. Finish your boxes with French polish, rubbed oil, Danish oil, carnauba wax, or leave them plain.

Lantern Case

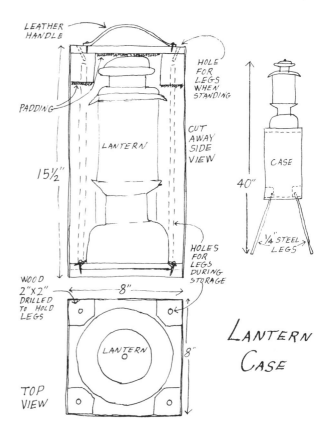

LANTERN CASE

The gasoline lantern is one of the few inventions of modern civilization that can truthfully be said to have penetrated to the ends of the earth. I have sat beside their bright light in expedition huts on the Arctic tundra, on mounds of pounded coral beneath coconut palms in Polynesia, in an isolated Finnish farmhouse, in dirt-floored peon homes in Central America and on many camping trips throughout North America. However, this marvelous invention has two weak spots. The lantern's glass chimney and mineral-saturated silk mantle are both easily broken.

Some years ago I addressed this problem with a wood-and-metal box. It not only furnished protection for the lantern during storage and transit but it provided an elevated stand for camp use when no table or tree was available. Shortly after making this container I was camping with friends in the Sierras when an engineer saw my creation and called it a "transtainer." He said it meant a transportation container. That's the perfect term for this project, and others in this book. I made this transtainer with wooden parts and an aluminum skin, but pressed wood or thin plywood could have been used for the skin. Some fine battery-powered, fluorescent lanterns are now on the market. If you have one of these, just design your lamp case for its size and shape.

The figures given are for the large-size, Coleman white, gasoline lantern. If your lantern is different be sure to adjust your measurements to fit.

I made the bottom of the case, to which the lantern is attached, from two thicknesses of ½-inch plywood. In the top of these I cut a hole the size of the lantern base. The lantern base fits into this and is held with round-headed wood screws with washers. The top is made from one piece of ½-inch plywood. I glued a piece of 2-inch stock on the underside of this with a hole to accommodate the top of the lantern. Both of these pieces are padded where they make contact with the lantern. The corners of the transtainer are reinforced with 2 by 2-inch pieces with their inner corner planed off. I drilled these to hold the four legs which are ¼-inch steel rods 13½ inches long. The aluminum skin is attached to the top and corner reinforcements with countersunk flat-headed wood screws. The top has a leather carrying handle as well as four holes to hold the legs at an angle of about 72 degrees.

The bottom, with the attached lantern, is held in the case with eight pins 2 inches long made from 20-penny nails. They are held in the plywood bottom by friction. I painted the legs bright yellow to prevent their loss while in camp. The other wood parts were also painted. If you use pressed board or plywood for the skin, four pieces will be needed. The corners could be mitred or butt joints could be used.

Although the lantern case offers a lot of protection I find it a good idea to tape a spare package of mantles inside. I find it easier to pack and unpack this transtainer in an upside-down position. When the case and legs are used to support the lantern in camp the lantern top is 40 inches above the ground.

Birch-Bark Boxes

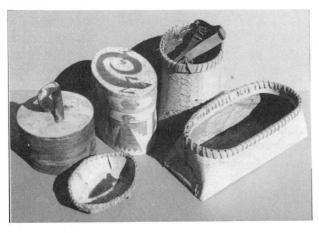

Any tree that gives us such diverse products as plywood, toothpicks, and canoes has got to be a special gift from nature. Birch bark is light, strong, flexible, and waterproof, which makes it a choice material from which to craft a box. These attributes were not lost on our ancestors, from Native Americans to Scandinavian artists, who utilized it in many ways. Five boxes are shown in the photo. The round-lidded box is made in a Scandinavian style, while the oval-lidded box is a modern style even though the designs are of Southwest Indian origin. The three boxes without lids are all authentic Native American types.

The paper or white birch is native to the areas north and east of the Great Lakes but it has been widely planted in other places. Before harvesting any bark please reread the section on this subject in the introduction. Birchbark is best worked when green, but if dry it can be softened by soaking in cool water for a few days. It can also be thinned by peeling away inner or outer layers. This procedure can also be used to bring out the various colors that range from off-white to tan to

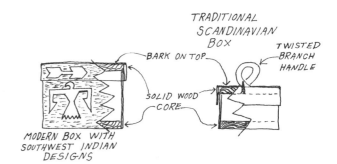

reddish brown. To make any box from bark, first lay out the design in pencil and then cut it out with craft shears or a pocket knife.

The Scandinavian and modern boxes both use a solid-wood insert for the body and lid. The bark is wrapped around this core and attached with either white or yellow glue. While drying, the bark can be held in place with cord, stout rubber bands, or hose clamps. The top of the lids on both of these boxes is covered with bark. On the Scandinavian box the lid is covered with the white outer bark while on the body the reddish inner

A birch-bark overlay ready to be cemented to the body of the box.

Lid and lid side of Birch-Bark Box about to be glued.

bark is used to achieve color contrast. The box's handle is made of twisted branch. The box of Southwest Indian design is done with an overlay technique. The bark is first split, then the pattern is cut out of the outer layer and the two pieces are put together with contact cement. This piece is then glued to form the box. This appliqué method can be used for all manner of decorating on birch-bark containers. These two boxes are made essentially like the bentwood box dealt with earlier in this chapter.

The boxes without lids are all authentic Indian designs and are stitched with spruce root. These are roots about ⅛ inch in diameter that can be found by running your hand into the soft duff that accumulates in spruce forests. If you take only one or two from a tree you will do it no harm. Working with spruce roots is a bit like working with willow twigs in basket making. First the bark and side rootlets are scraped away. If the root is too thick it can be split in half or even into quarters with a pocket knife and these pieces can be scraped until they are round or oval in cross section.

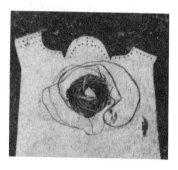

Birch bark cut to box shape, with a supply of spruce root for lacing.

The actual stitching is simple because the end of the root can be shaped to a point thus forming a needle. The root can be used green or after soaking in water if it has dried out. Holes can be made in the bark with a leather punch or an awl for the stitching. Be careful when sewing because the stitches can easily pull through the bark in one direction. Just as in basketry, when the end of a root is reached it is tucked in, out of sight, and a new length is started.

The shallow, bark container with the arrowhead is the sort of box that an Indian might have whipped up in half an hour to hold berries or nuts that were being gathered. It is made from a roughly circular piece of bark stitched to a light wooden hoop. Cuts are made along the radii and the bark overlapped, thus allowing the rim to turn

up. The pattern for the other two is a bit more involved and is shown in the drawing. These two boxes require the sewing of an end seam and flap. Note that on the shallow box the flap is on the inside while on the tall model it is on the outside. A leather handle is included on the tall box.

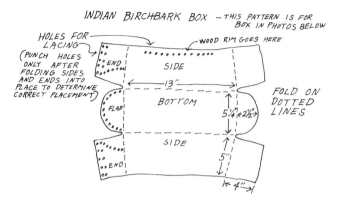

End of an authentic Indian Birch-Bark Box being stitched with spruce root.

Stitching the rim of a Birch-Bark Box.

I normally leave my Birch-Bark Boxes in their natural state so the swirls and flecks can show through, but if you anticipate a great deal of handling for a particular box you may want to apply some finish. If you cannot acquire the bark of the paper birch I suggest you experiment with the local species. And if you don't have a supply of spruce roots handy try substituting leather lacing, raffia, or waxed cord.

Sculptured-Lid Dovetail Box

Here is a strong, good-looking box that has many uses, or it can stand alone as a conversation piece. It was made from black walnut, hard maple, and sugar pine. Its two unique features are its sculptured lid and the dovetail joints on the box corners. You may want to consider both of these ideas for other box projects. I am not a big fan of the dovetail joint, but I acknowledge it as a strong and beautiful joint and must admit that no book on boxes would be complete without its inclusion. On the rare occasion when I use this joint I make it by hand, and that is the method I will describe here. For production work, however, a high-quality router and two dovetail jigs are the answer. The two jigs are needed so you can move

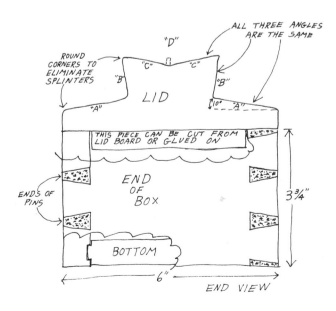

quickly between the two cuts. My chief tools are a small backsaw with 35 teeth per inch and a blade thickness of 16 thousandths of an inch, and a ½-inch bevelled chisel. Some readers, I am sure, are experts at this joint but for those who are not I'll explain my methods.

Making Dovetail Joints

Before I go into the specific steps, here are a few general remarks on making a dovetail joint. I make all marks either with the fine point on my marking gauge or with a thin-pointed awl. A pencil mark is way too wide for accuracy and I find knife-made lines too hard to see. An ordinary backsaw can be used to make this joint but it takes a master woodworker to get satisfactory re-

Dovetail joints and some of the tools used to fashion them.

sults with such a tool. I recommend the thinnest bladed and finest toothed backsaw you can find. Concentrate on making the saw cuts accurate and the remainder of the joint will fall into place. I saw on the waste side of my scribed lines. Be sure your chisels are razor sharp. Most experts do the cleanup on pins and tails with a chisel and I sometimes use this tool but I also like a sharp pocketknife for this job. The parts of this joint are always identified by looking at the long grain of the wood. The pins have parallel sides just like the sides of a straight pin and the tails have a decidedly flared-out, bird-tail look about them. As on any piece of accurate woodworking be sure you have good light, measure carefully and always double-check before cutting, and color-in the waste areas to be removed.

Here are my steps for making a dovetail joint:
1. Use wood of the same thickness and width. Square and dress it on all sides.

2. Set the marking gauge 1/32-inch thicker than the wood and mark the ends of all the pieces.
3. Next lay out the pins as shown in the drawing.
4. Saw the end grain down to the mark, then allow the chisel to drop into the scribe mark and

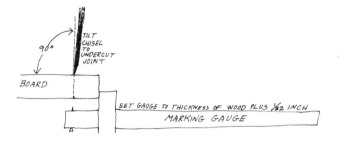

cut out the waste between the pins. Hold the chisel a few degrees off of perpendicular and work from both sides. Clean up the cuts.
5. To mark the tails clamp the pin piece to the side and mark the tail cuts from the inside with an awl. Using a try square extend these marks across the end grain.

Dovetail Joints

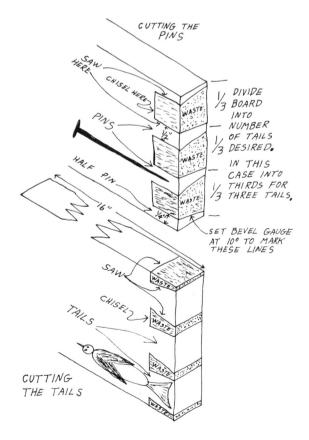

6. To form the tails first saw down to the mark and then chisel out the waste. Tilt the chisel a few degrees as before.
7. Test-fit the joint. It should be snug but not tight to the point that solid blows are demanded to drive it home. When you are happy with the fit apply glue.

Sculpting the Lid

This sculptured lid utilizes the very same angles as the dovetail joints. I left my bevel gauge at 10 degrees and marked the cuts for the lid. Cuts "A" and "B" were simple to make on the table saw with the blade tilted 10 degrees. However, my blade was not large enough to make the cuts marked "C". This could probably be done with a router but I made the shallow saw cut at "D" and used a chisel and plane to remove the unwanted wood.

This box was purposely made long and narrow so the sculptured lid would be easy to grasp. Other dimensions would naturally have been satisfactory but I find a container of this shape quite handy. I used tung oil for the finish.

Stamp Caddy

This is one of the smallest boxes in this book and one of the simplest to make. It is also one of the handiest projects, solving that common problem of loose or lost postage stamps. As both the United States and Canadian Post Offices sell stamps in coils, the Stamp Caddy is a neat way to dispense them. Too, a stamp caddy made from attractive woods is a nice addition to any desktop. These are such a snap to make and so appreciated as gifts that I often make a number of them at one time. Only four pieces of wood are needed and chances are you have some great-looking scrap that will fill the bill.

A number of hardwoods were used to make these three Stamp Caddies.

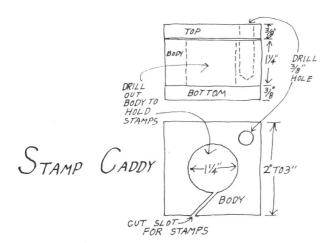

Needle Box

To make a stamp caddy, first find a piece of wood for the body that measures 2 to 3 inches on a side and is 1¼ inches thick. Second, drill a hole 1¼ inches in diameter in the middle of this piece. If you are making a number of caddies drill all the holes at the same time. Third, with a fine-toothed backsaw, cut through the side of this piece as shown in the drawing. Fourth, secure some wood ¼ to ⅜ inch in thickness and saw it into squares the size of your caddies. You will need two pieces for each caddy. Fifth, glue one of these pieces to the bottom of the caddy. Sixth,

Stamp Caddies under construction. Note the bottom already glued in place.

clamp the other square on top of the caddy and drill a ⅜-inch hole through this piece and three-quarters of the way into the corner of the body. Seventh, glue a 1-inch piece of ⅜-inch dowel into the hole in the top. To assemble the caddy push the dowel that protrudes from the top into the body of the box. Finally, sand all of the surfaces and finish with carnauba paste wax. The wax finish is important on this project because it lubricates the lid and the dowel when they are pivoted to insert a new coil of stamps.

If you were to ask three people what a needle box looks like you could well receive three answers. One would describe a small box to hold sewing needles while the other two might mention containers for crochet or knitting needles. They would, of course, all be correct and this versatile, sliding-top box can be made in sizes to accommodate any of these items. It's also a good container for pencils, harmonica, dominos, checkers, chopsticks, and playing cards.

There are many ways of making sliding wood lids and if you have a favorite method you may not be interested in my technique, but I find it an easy and fast method. It's done on the table saw with a thin kerf, carbide-tipped blade. Both the rim and sliding lid are cut from the same piece with two passes through the saw, which is set at an angle of 10 to 12 degrees. I saw off the two rim pieces from the edge of the lid without changing the rip fence. The drawing shows this procedure. When these rim pieces are cut free

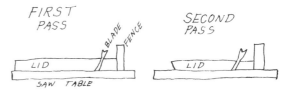

they are trapped between the turning blade and the fence and could shoot backwards. Being aware of this danger, I stay out of harm's way and have never had a problem. If you heed my warning and only do this cut when you are alert and not likely to be distracted you should have no difficulties.

The two rim pieces are glued back to the lid with a piece of veneer inserted to give the lid clearance to slide freely. You can use commercial

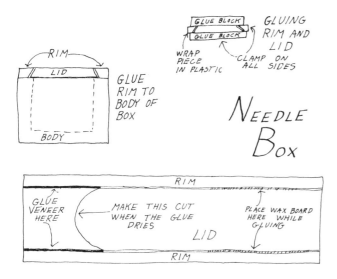

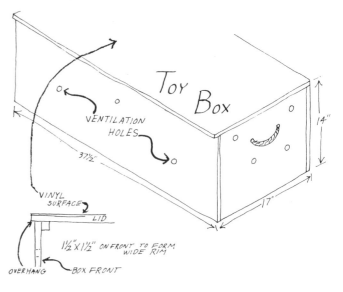

veneer of the same color or purposely use a contrasting color. If you want a perfect match, saw a piece 1/32 of an inch thick from your stock. I place strips of wax board, cut from a milk carton, between these three pieces when I glue them to keep everything parallel and to provide clearance. When the glue dries I cut the lid free with a coping saw and glue the rim in place atop the box. To hollow out the body of these boxes I use the techniques described in band-saw or drilled boxes. Lastly, the box and lid are sanded and finished with paste wax. This is a fine finish for items that are often handled and it serves as a lubricant for the lid as well.

Toy Box

The Toy Box shown here is a rather plain affair. If you decide to make this project you may want to

jazz yours up with colorful ducks, elephants, flowers, or other such motifs. The point of this design is not its attractiveness but its many safety and practical features.

First, the lid is covered with tough floor vinyl so it will withstand pounding and the other abuse that Toy Box tops are subject to. Second, it is a low box so that youngsters can use it as a seat or workbench. Third, the lid is made of 1/2-inch plywood without a frame. This means it is quite light and not likely to hurt little fingers if it closes on them. To enhance this safety feature the body of the box has a wide rim so there is no cutting edge. Fourth, as youngsters have a way of getting trapped in boxes, this design has ventilation holes drilled on all sides. Also, there is no latch of any kind. Fifth, there is no handle on the lid to interfere with it, serving as a work space. Instead, the lid clears the front of the box sufficiently to provide a grip. Finally, the handles at the ends of the box are made of rope to prevent bruised knees and shins.

The construction is of the simplest six-board type, using 1/2-inch plywood for the front, back, and lid and 3/4-inch plywood for the ends and bottom. White glue and countersunk finishing nails hold things together. The lid is held in place with a long section of piano hinge. The vinyl, a scrap from one of our floors, is held in place with contact cement. All of the box, except the vinyl, was given two coats of polyurethane. The handles are 1/2-inch Manila hemp spliced inside the box.

In & Out Boxes

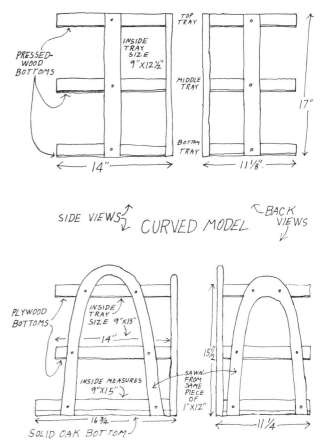

STRAIGHT MODEL

PRESSED-WOOD BOTTOMS

INSIDE TRAY SIZE 9"X12½"

TOP TRAY

MIDDLE TRAY

BOTTOM TRAY

17"

14"

11⅛"

SIDE VIEWS   CURVED MODEL   BACK VIEWS

PLYWOOD BOTTOMS

INSIDE TRAY SIZE 9"X13"

14"

INSIDE MEASURES 9"X15"

16¾

SOLID OAK BOTTOM

15½

SAWN FROM SAME PIECE OF 1"X12"

11¼

This item has probably provided more material for cartoonists than any other desktop accessory. That notwithstanding, I find it a very useful item as well as a fun, one-evening project. These boxes are so easy to craft that you may want to make some as gifts for friends—from paper-pushing bureaucrats to hassled executives. Two designs are shown.

One set was made with straight oak frames on pressed-wood tray bottoms. It was put together with wood screws and glue. This is a simple, straightforward design but it is also quite functional. Unless you really load the trays down with heavy stuff, the two-point suspension on each tray is adequate.

The other design utilizes a curved frame and four-point suspension for each tray. Both of these curved supports are band-sawed from one piece of 1 by 12. The highest curve also provides a handle for the In & Out Box. This unit was fashioned from a mixture of woods, has ¼-inch plywood bottoms for the upper trays, and was stained.

The measurements given are to accommodate standard 8½ by 11 typing paper. If you want to use your boxes for legal-sized paper, add three inches to the long dimension on the trays. If you plan to employ the trays for other purposes, you can adjust the dimensions accordingly. Both of these designs have been made with three trays, which I refer to as "In," "Out," and "Other," but, of course, you can make yours with two trays or even four or five. You can have a good time coming up with wild designs. I finished mine with polyurethane.

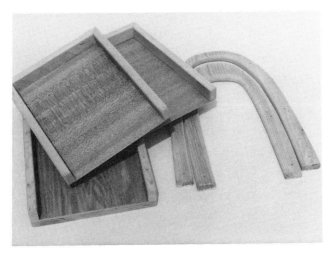

Parts for a curved-frame In & Out Box.

Display Boxes

Only two rather different boxes are shown here but I'm sure you can expand on these ideas and come up with other models to display miscellanea you have made, found, collected, or earned. Naturally, sizes will vary depending on the items to be displayed. I have a general theory that boxes of this sort should be kept plain so as not to detract from the items being shown. Both of these boxes follow that view.

The first box is made from thin plywood and is much like the front and back cover of a large book. The wood margin around these pieces provides some depth so patches and pins can be mounted. The display surface is a layer of sheet cork covered with felt. Items can be mounted with small pins or tacks or by using the method described in the Shadow Box project. When this box is slightly open it is freestanding, so the display can be positioned almost anywhere. When closed and secured with large rubber bands the box protects the contents during transit or storage.

The second Display Box is made much like a picture frame. It has a solid wood frame with a ridged, clear-plastic front. Display items like sea shells, coins, barbed wire, knives, or arrowheads are placed on the plastic from the rear. They are given a backdrop of felt or other suitable fabric, then a layer of batting, and finally a piece of plywood or cardboard that is secured by brads that are driven into the sides of the box. Either of these boxes is ideal for displaying items that are too thick for presentation in an album.

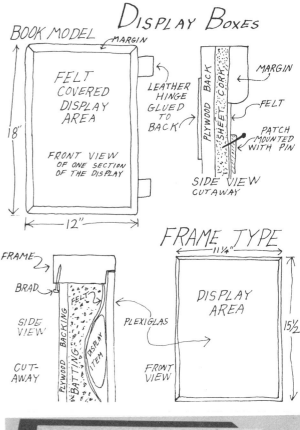

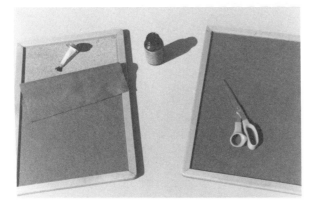

Gluing felt over the cork backing on a book-type Display Box.

A picture-frame-style Display Box being measured for its plastic front.

Under-Bed Storage Drawer

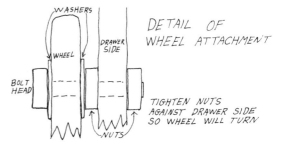

The wheels are assembled by passing the bolt through a washer, then the wheel and another washer. Next, a nut is screwed on and the bolt end is pushed through the hole in the side of the drawer. Finally, the second nut is tightened on the inside of the drawer to secure the wheel in place.

"We don't have enough storage space." I've heard that remark often and I'll bet you have too. Perhaps you have even uttered those very words. One storage area often overlooked is the space under a bed. A storage drawer converts that area into a convenient and organized place for all manner of household items. Our children found these especially handy and I'm sure yours will also.

The Under-Bed Storage Drawer rolls on four wooden wheels band-sawed from 1-inch stock. They are 4 inches in diameter and fasten to the drawer with machine bolts. One extra nut is needed for each bolt as well as two washers. All together you will need four bolts about 2½ inches long, eight nuts, and eight washers. Bolts with a diameter of ⅜ of an inch will do fine. The drawer, which is essentially a box, is constructed of 1 by 6 stock and the bottom of ⅜- or ½-inch plywood. Fasten all the wooden parts together with yellow glue and wood screws and add a handle to the front.

A wheel and assembly being tightened on an Under-Bed Storage Box.

Although I have given dimensions on the drawing, it is important to measure the available space under each bed and adjust the size to fit. For large beds it's best to have a smaller drawer on each side rather than one giant drawer. Two coats of polyurethane provide a suitable finish.

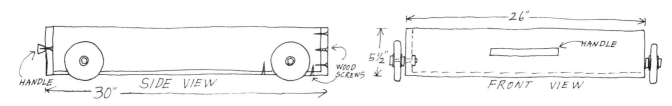

Pioneer Trunk

Remember the old movies that featured wagon trains plodding slowly across the Great Plains? Invariably the settlers tried to carry too much in their prairie schooners and, when the way became hard, the trail would be littered with bureaus, rocking chairs, and the like. But, as I remember, these pioneers always retained a medium-size trunk that would yield up all manner of needed items. Many of these old trunks were of a very practical design, at once roomy, sturdy, and good-looking. Traditionally the sides of these trunks were straight and the top rounded. Compared to either the Pirate or Sailors Chest this trunk seems somewhat plain, but the hide covering and the brass-tack designs give it a homespun appeal. I based the size of this project on an average from two old trunks I had the opportunity to measure.

I used a combination of old and new material to make my trunk. The two ends are Philippine mahogany while the front and back are of plywood. I placed the best face of the plywood on the inside because I knew the outside would be covered. The lower portion of the trunk is basic six-board construction held together with yellow glue and nails. To form the lid I placed a ledge of plywood inside the mahogany ends. This ledge has the same curve as the mahogany ends but is 1 inch lower, thus forming a shelf. The pieces that formed the curved top rested on this shelf at both ends. They too were held in place with yellow glue and nails. Be sure no nail heads stick up. If

**Partially completed
Pioneer Trunk.**

PIONEER TRUNK

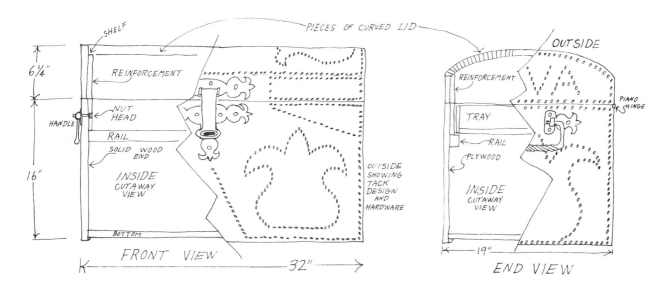

FRONT VIEW

END VIEW

you like making the shavings fly, as I do, you will enjoy the next job, that of planing down the lid. The outside need not be pretty, only correctly rounded, as it will be covered with hide. I spent more time smoothing the inside of the lid because I knew it would show when open. The lid is a full inch thick for strength and attached with a piano hinge.

Using a scorp to shave the inside lid of the Pioneer Trunk.

My trunk was covered with untanned cowhide (with the hair on) that I purchased from a rancher. Rawhide, that is, untanned cowhide with the hair removed and planed to a uniform thickness, is available at any good leather store and is the covering I would recommend. It is just as authentic and, because of its uniform thickness, it is much

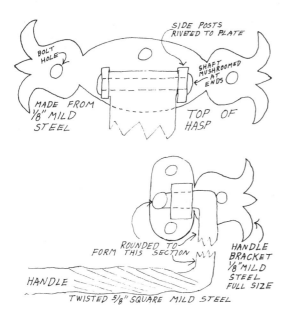

easier to use. For a Pioneer Trunk of this size you will need a full hide from a medium-size steer. You can work the rawhide wet, by bending it around corners and tacking it in place, or you can use it dry. To do this, lay out the pattern on the hide in pencil, then cut the pieces with craft shears and fasten them to the trunk with contact cement. In both cases the decorative tacks are added later.

Brass-headed upholstering tacks are the traditional way to decorate these trunks. You can use any design that appeals to you and incorporate dates, names, initials, logos, brands, etc. I employed a three-pointed tulip design for both the brass-tack decorations and my homemade hardware. See the technical notes earlier in this chapter regarding sources of hardware.

When the rawhide was all tacked in place I attached the handles and hasp with ¼-inch carriage bolts. I reinforced the inside of the trunk where the hardware was bolted and countersunk the nuts. I equipped this trunk with a half shelf that slides on rails, and finished the inside with two coats of spar urethane.

Fireplace Wood Box

Most boxes that I have seen for holding firewood were plain rectangular affairs. I am sure these did the job for which they were designed but when I was asked by my nephew to build one for his new home I decided on a design with more flair. My open styling may hardly fit the definition of a box but it certainly does the job of a box so I'm including it in this chapter.

I employed the simplest construction possible,

having two 2 by 4-inch purlins extend the length of the box for a foundation. The bottom consists of 2-inch lumber fastened to the purlins with 16-penny nails. Lumber 2 inches thick is also used for the ends. It is supported by four braces made from mild steel measuring ⅜ by 1½ inches. The braces are screwed to the bottom crosspieces and then the sides are fastened in place with wood screws from the outside. I painted the screw heads black so they match the black steelwork perfectly.

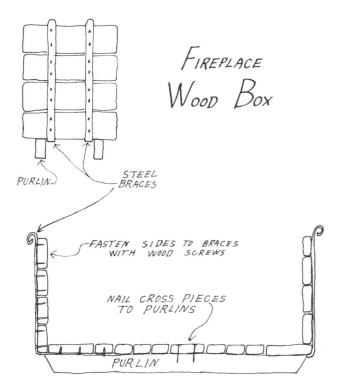

FIREPLACE
WOOD BOX

PURLIN

STEEL BRACES

FASTEN SIDES TO BRACES WITH WOOD SCREWS

NAIL CROSS PIECES TO PURLINS

PURLIN

The making of these four braces is a good beginner's blacksmithing project so you may want to try it. The end of each piece of steel is drawn out and curled and then the 90-degree bend is made to form the brace. If you decide to give smithing a try I suggest you reread the technical notes on the topic earlier. If you decide not to make these ends you can have a local blacksmith make them for you or hunt around for some prebent pieces that will do the job. This project lends itself to many variations in size and style. One side could be higher than the other, for example, or a back could be included, or a small box for kindling attached to one end. Naturally this project can be finished to complement its surroundings.

Kyack Box

During my first summer at Philmont Scout Ranch in the mountains of New Mexico I took two groups of Explorer Scouts on six-week hiking trips into the highest and wildest parts of the property. During part of each trip we used pack burros. This necessitated my signing out for these hay burners and their tack. One of the items checked out was a set of kyack boxes. Having at one time during my youth been half owner of a kayak, I knew what that was but I didn't fathom "kyack boxes." They turned out to be a set of sturdy boxes made to be slung on either side of the burro's pack saddle.

I have been exposed to a great deal of animal packing since that initiation many years ago and have gained a lot of respect for pack animals and their impedimenta. When you travel deep into the back country with pack animals you leave behind many of the trappings of more luxurious campgrounds—like picnic tables. So when I decided to make a set of kyack boxes I wanted to incorporate a camp table. This was not to be a sit-down-type table but rather a work area for the all-important cook. The entire equation is further complicated because these containers had to be rugged enough to stand up to the jarring that anything on a horse or burro receives, but also relatively light in weight.

My solution was to build a set of boxes of plywood with sides that folded out to form the tabletop when camp was set up. Dowel legs fit into brackets on the box ends to elevate the table. The box sides are held out like table wings, with braces. Kyack Boxes are always made in pairs so

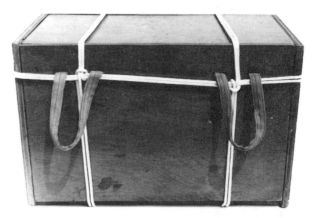

Tied-up Kyack Box ready to be slung on a horse's pack saddle.

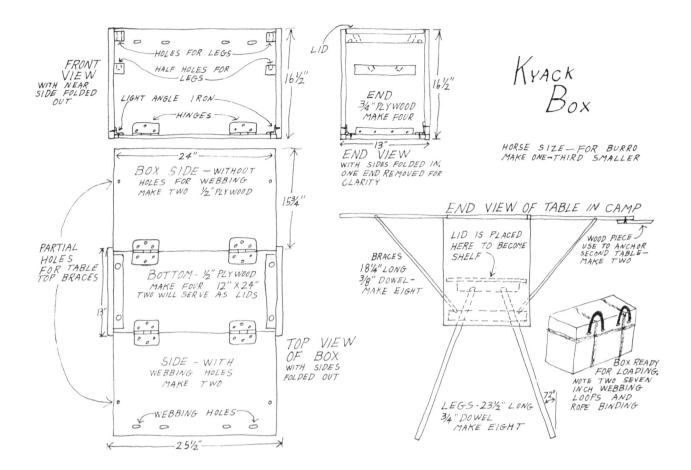

FRONT VIEW
WITH NEAR SIDE FOLDED OUT

HOLES FOR LEGS
HALF HOLES FOR LEGS
LIGHT ANGLE IRON
HINGES

16½"

LID

END
¾" PLYWOOD
MAKE FOUR

16½"

END VIEW
WITH SIDES FOLDED IN, ONE END REMOVED FOR CLARITY

13"

KYACK BOX

HORSE SIZE—FOR BURRO MAKE ONE-THIRD SMALLER

24"

BOX SIDE — WITHOUT HOLES FOR WEBBING MAKE TWO ½" PLYWOOD

15¾"

PARTIAL HOLES FOR TABLE TOP BRACES

BOTTOM — ½" PLYWOOD MAKE FOUR 12" X 24" TWO WILL SERVE AS LIDS

13"

SIDE — WITH WEBBING HOLES MAKE TWO

WEBBING HOLES

25½"

TOP VIEW OF BOX
WITH SIDES FOLDED OUT

END VIEW OF TABLE IN CAMP

LID IS PLACED HERE TO BECOME SHELF

WOOD PIECE USE TO ANCHOR SECOND TABLE— MAKE TWO

BRACES 18¼" LONG ⅜" DOWEL— MAKE EIGHT

BOX READY FOR LOADING. NOTE TWO SEVEN INCH WEBBING LOOPS AND ROPE BINDING

72°

LEGS - 23½" LONG ¾" DOWEL MAKE EIGHT

Braces and legs convert a Kyack Box into a table, shown lying on its side.

Kyack Box with one side open. Note leg and brace.

that the pack animal can be fitted with a balanced load. In camp I usually fasten both tables together, with small pieces of wood screwed into place, to form a sizable cook's work area.

To construct this project, first fashion all of the parts as shown in the drawing, including fastening the braces to the box ends. Then attach the box ends to the bottom using light but strong angle irons. Next attach the two sides to the bottom with sturdy hinges. I employed wood screws, nails, and glue to hold my boxes together and finished them with three coats of spar urethane.

A Kyack Box is fastened to a pack saddle by two loops. I used extremely strong nylon webbing to make these loops. An overhand knot is placed at one end of a 55-inch piece of webbing. It is threaded through the four holes to form two outside loops and is tied off with another overhand knot. The top and sides of the box are held closed with rope during transit. Carry the dowels in a cloth bag inside one of the boxes along with your camp gear.

Blanket Chest

If I remember correctly, about one fourth of the students in my high-school shop class made cedar chests for their mothers. I didn't, but when I built our master-bedroom addition my wife allowed as how a Blanket Chest would be a desirable item for the room. Some years before, I had purchased some fine squares of red lauan and had carved fleur-de-lis on two of these. When I thought of incorporating these carvings in the chest I decided I needed two more, so I did the same relief carving

on the other side and sawed the squares apart. This provided a carving for each end and two for the front. I still thought the front needed a little something more so I did the Maltese Cross in maple as a contrasting motif.

The cedar chests I remember from high school were of six-board construction using panels of

A detailed view of a carving used on the Blanket Chest.

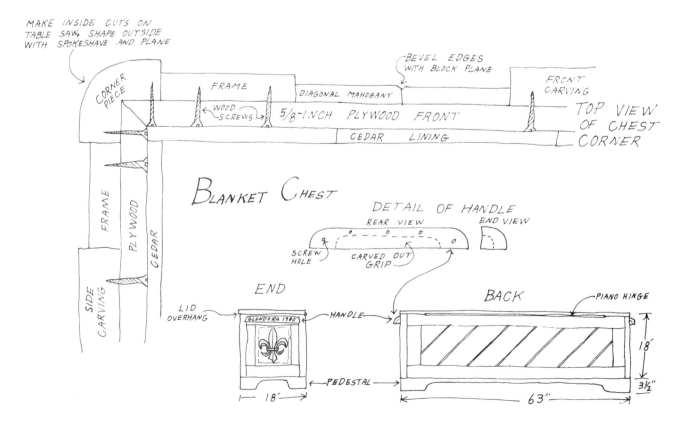

glued-up eastern red cedar. To utilize my carvings I employed an entirely different method for making my panels. Each panel was made of ⅝-inch plywood with an apitong frame. On the top and back this panel is filled in with diagonal pieces of Philippine mahogany ½ inch thick. The same procedure was used on the ends and front except that the carvings were included.

The ¾-inch bottom is supported by a low pedestal with legs at each corner. Four rounded corner braces are screwed to the bottom and the side panels are fitted between these and secured with wood screws from the inside. The interior of the chest was completely sheathed with aromatic red cedar, which was not coated with any finish. The rim of the chest was dressed up with thin strips of mahogany and the lid was attached with a long piece of piano hinge. The lid overhangs the front panel just enough to allow a fingerhold for easy opening. Carved handles were attached to each end and the chest was given two coats of polyurethane.

The Blanket Chest measures 63 by 18 by 18 inches, which makes it a large project for a small shop. However, my construction method yielded an unexpected dividend. Although some of the panels were large they were light in weight and could easily be stored out of the way if I wanted to do other jobs. So I only had to deal with the full-size chest during its final assembly. This method of building large boxes from plywood panels, and the idea of covering these panels with carvings and/or thin wood strips, both lend themselves to use on many other projects.

Scandinavian Seaman's Chest

Here is a container that has a distinctive shape with plenty of flare, great possibilities for colorful decoration, and an exciting history. Its bloodlines

represent the need of those who go down to the sea in ships for dry, secure storage for their personal items. Thousands of these chests were made during the days of "wooden ships and iron men." They accompanied sailors on voyages of adventure to every saltwater port on the globe.

These Seaman's Chests were normally not large because space in the crew's quarters was limited. Two chests were usually stored under the lower berth of a double bunk. They were flat-topped so they could be pulled out and used for seating. Each country used different designs but they were usually resplendent with bright colors perhaps to remind a lonely sailor on a cold, gray day of the verdant flora and blossoms of home. I have decorated my chest with a combination of traditional and modern Scandinavian designs.

I started by cutting out the two end pieces and essentially built the chest around these. The ends are panels of ½-inch wood on the outside glued to ½-inch plywood. Most of this project is made from ½-inch Philippine mahogany salvaged from pallets. I put the body of the chest together first

Bottom of Seaman's Chest being nailed in place.

Gluing the lid of the Seaman's Chest.

and then constructed the lid, ending with the top bevel pieces. Yellow glue and 2-inch finish nails were used to hold everything together. One different feature on this chest is the drop on the front edge of the lid which fits into a swale in the rim.

I did this here so the lock set I wanted to use would fit, but this feature is not uncommon on old chests. Presumably this is done as a point of decoration or to add strength to the lid. However, don't feel that you must copy this feature. After

Seaman's Chest

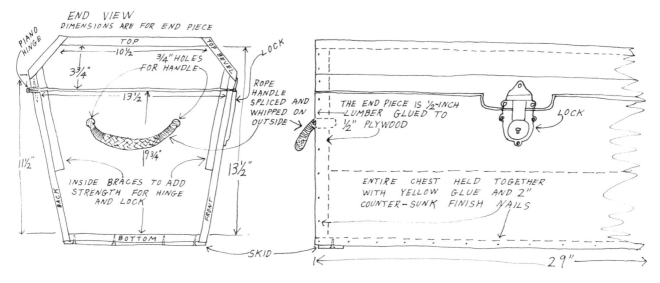

END VIEW
DIMENSIONS ARE FOR END PIECE

PIANO HINGE

TOP

10½

3¾

3¾" HOLES FOR HANDLE

13½

TOP BEVEL

LOCK

ROPE HANDLE SPLICED AND WHIPPED ON OUTSIDE

9¾

11½

INSIDE BRACES TO ADD STRENGTH FOR HINGE AND LOCK

BACK

FRONT

13½"

BOTTOM

SKID

THE END PIECE IS ½-INCH LUMBER GLUED TO ½" PLYWOOD

LOCK

ENTIRE CHEST HELD TOGETHER WITH YELLOW GLUE AND 2" COUNTER-SUNK FINISH NAILS

29"

Completed Seaman's Chest before painting.

do one color each day it's amazing how fast the painting gets done. If your regular job is during the day, painting one color at a time is a good evening task. Lastly, I added two varnished oak skids.

The rope handles definitely add a nautical touch to this chest. Even if you have never spliced a rope before, I urge you to try your hand at this useful skill. The rope handles could have simply been knotted on the inside of the chest but I decided a short splice would be more authentic. You

drilling ¾-inch holes for the handles I sanded the chest and gave it a primer coat and two finish coats of paint. I mixed the finish coat from several pigments, striving to achieve a bright rose red.

Suitable designs are to be found in books on folk art. I endeavored to stick to Scandinavian motifs but Pennsylvania Dutch or modern nautical designs are other possibilities. I use oil-base enamels with small brushes. By working toward myself and always keeping my wrist steadied in front of the work I keep the design accurate. My normal practice is to do one panel at a time. If I

START OF SHORT SPLICE

PUSH ROPE TOGETHER AND WEAVE ENDS UNDER SHADED AREAS

EACH END SHOULD BE WOVEN UNDER THREE TIMES

WHIPPING THE ENDS OF SPLICE

LOOP

USE STRONG WAXED CORD FOR WHIPPING

START OF WHIPPING OPERATION

END OF WHIPPING OPERATION

LOOP

PULL CORD UNTIL LOOP IS PULLED INTO HERE

Rope handle on the Seaman's Chest with half the splice completed.

Views of completed Pirate Chests: (*above*) made of mixed wood, (*right*) oak.

will find this craft illustrated in most books dealing with knots and splices. The basic idea of the short splice is to unravel about 4 inches from both ends of a 24-inch piece of ½-inch rope. These ends are placed together as shown in the drawing and the ends are then woven back into the standing parts of the rope in a basic over–under pattern. Weave each end under three strands of the rope and the splice is complete. To neaten the rope fibres sticking out from the splice I whipped each end of the splice with waxed linen cord. The sketch will give you a few clues on how to do this. If you have trouble with splicing or whipping, ask a Boy Scout for help.

Pirate Chest

I've saved this project for the end of this chapter, not because it is the most beautiful or the heaviest but rather because it, more than any other project, brought about this book. After finishing my second Pirate Chest the inspiration hit me that this could be the linchpin for a volume on boxes and such.

The Pirate Chest has such rakish lines that you may want to build one just for its conversation appeal. It is a fantastic woodworking project, with angles and curves aplenty, and it provides storage space as well. Sawing the precision angles for the chest is fun, but shaping the inside and outside of the lid is pure delight. The shavings fall like rain and those gorgeous curves come alive beneath your tools like magic. I have never figured out why pirates came up with a chest with such flair, but I'm glad they did.

Pirate Chests lend themselves to treatment in many sizes from small jewelry boxes to full-size models suitable for burying treasure on desert islands. So your first job is to decide on a size and to work up a template for the ends. The entire project is constructed around the ends, so this step is important. I have used an angle of 83 degrees on this chest but you can vary that a few degrees if you like. Just keep drawing until you achieve a shape you like. Next glue up the panels for the front, back, bottom, and ends, and saw them to shape. The drawing on the next page is of a chest of mixed wood 2 inches thick and with handmade hardware. The slightly smaller chest in the photo above right is of oak a full inch thick and utilizes commercial hardware.

With your table saw set at 83 degrees you next cut the edges of the front, back, and bottom. The bottom edge of the front and back of the lid can also be sawn at this time. Next saw the end pieces in two and attach the bottom, front, and back to the lower portion of the ends. On this chest I did this with yellow glue and handmade nails with large showy heads. On the oak chest, sheet-metal screws were used. These were covered with contrasting wooden plugs.

To fashion the lid, first attach the front and back pieces to the upper portion of the ends. To cover the remainder of this complex curve I use my table saw to cut truncated triangles that are the length of the chest, then glue them in place. I

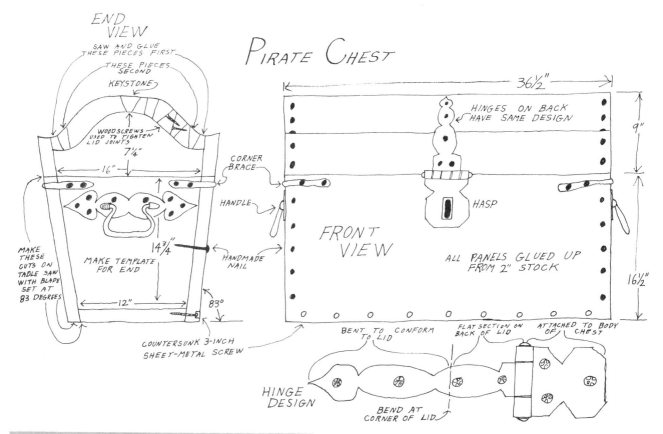

Plenty of clamps are needed to construct a lid for a Pirate Chest.

work from both the front and back and use wood screws where necessary to hold these strips in place. Be sure that any screws used are placed in the center of these strips so your tools cannot possibly strike them when you plane the lid. Don't worry at this time about the inside and outside of the lid being uneven because that will be planed down later. The last lid piece to be fitted in place is ideally a keystone-shaped piece that is glued on the apex of the lid.

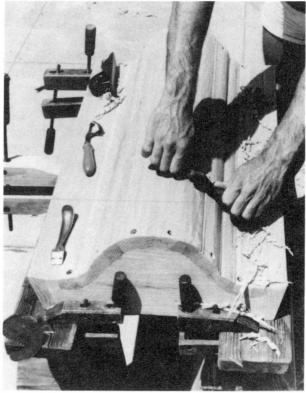

Using a spokeshave to shape the lid of a Pirate Chest.

To me one of the most enjoyable jobs in making a Pirate Chest is the shaping of the lid. You are right on top of the work and the chips just fly. I start by using a spokeshave and block plane on the convex curves which goes rather quickly. Then I proceed to the concave curves where I use a number of tools including curved adz, large gouges, a scorp, and especially spoon-bottom carving planes. This tool comes in push and pull designs and they both do a fine job. Because working room is more restricted on the inside of the lid, large gouges play a more important role. Curved scrapers and abrasive paper are used for the final smoothing.

On this chest I used handmade hinges to attach the lid while on the oak chest I used a long piece of piano hinge. The home-forged handles and hasp are shown in the photo. If you purchase handles for your chest be sure they are strong enough to lift the chest when it's loaded with treasure. The oak chest was stained first and then finished with spar urethane. The large chest has only a spar-urethane finish.

Body and lid of Pirate Chest before assembly, with hand- forged hardware in foreground.

BUCKETS

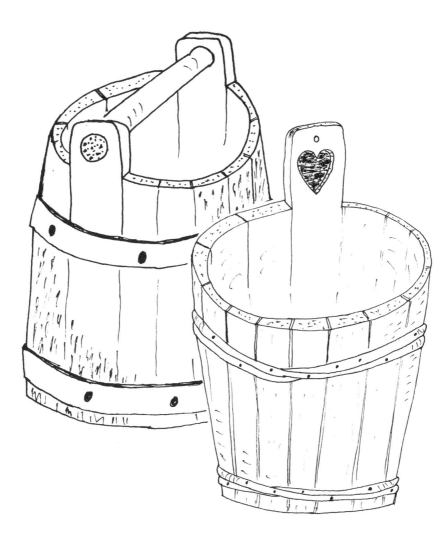

My guess is that most woodworkers have made some boxes and probably turned a few bowls, but I suspect that many have never made a bucket. If my guess is correct this section will cover new ground for most of you. The making of buckets, firkins, and piggins is a unique form of woodworking that is both challenging and fun. It differs from most woodworking in having few right angles. In fact, most of the pieces are curved or tapered on every surface. But what a thrill it is when these odd shapes come together to form a sturdy, attractive container.

Typical handmade cooperage: two Buckets (*top and bottom*), a Firkin (*center left*), and a Fruit Bowl (*center right*).

You might ask, why include such an unusual form of woodworking? To that, I have two answers. First, coopering is stand-up woodworking at its best. You work close to the wood and are treated to its aroma and feel as the shavings fly. Second, I have Swiss blood in my veins and Switzerland is possibly the cradle of stave-type coopering.

The beginnings of coopering are lost in antiquity but it is a very old and honored craft. The Greek historian Herodotus referred to barrels in the fifth century B.C. but these may have been hollowed-out palm trunks. However, the cooper and stave construction were well known by 500 A.D. The Roman scholar Pliny states that the first coopering was done in the Alps. This was a logical development to meet the need for strong, liquid-tight containers. Until glass bottles became generally available in the seventeen-hundreds, stave-built containers were used for storing and shipping most liquids and many dry products. Wooden barrels and kegs were widely used in the United States up until World War I. Since then, they have largely been replaced by metal, plastic, or cardboard containers. To me, the simple beauty of a coopered item in wood will never be duplicated by a mass-produced item. This is why I decided to try my hand at this ancient craft.

Too, some of my ancestors came from Switzerland, where they had a dairy farm. During the summer the herd of brown Swiss cows were taken to the high meadows where they ate well and produced prodigious amounts of milk. All of this liquid could not possibly be transported to the valley below so it was processed into more concentrated forms, namely butter and cheese. This work required all manner of buckets, tubs, and molds which were made by the farm families during the long winter evenings. So, in a small way, I suppose I come by my penchant for coopering naturally.

TYPES OF COOPERAGE

Wet cooperage is usually made of white oak which has closed cells and thus deters leakage. Can you imagine the chagrin of the first distiller who left his spirits to age in red oak barrels? Wet cooperage must be accurately made, and for hundreds of years represented the apex of the cooper's art. Besides spirits, these containers were used to store and ship wine, salted meat and fish, oil, vinegar, pickles, etc. They are still used extensively today to age premium wines and spirits. If you ever visit an old winery and see a giant coopered vat as big as a room that doesn't leak a drop, you are viewing a choice example of this respected craft.

Dry cooperage can be made from any reasonably strong wood with a bit of flexibility. Over the years these barrels and kegs have been used to store and transport flour, fruit, dried fish, chemicals, and nails. White cooperage is made from the various species of white pine. Its products were used primarily on the dairy farms of old. They are still made and sold as souvenirs in the mountainous areas of Central Europe.

A professional cooper has quite a collection of specialized tools. I had none of these when I first tried my hand at making a bucket but I got by and I suspect you will too. I am not a professional cooper, nor do I expect you to become one, but by following my amateur methods you should end up with professional results. So welcome to the old and honorable art of coopering!

TECHNICAL NOTES

The basic steps in making a wooden bucket, tub, firkin, or piggin are much the same so I'll cover them in some detail here and deal with specifics under individual projects.

I plan my cooperage projects by drawing a circle representing the top, outside diameter. For a first project I suggest a dimension of 10 to 12 inches. From this you can figure the number and width of staves as well as their edge angle. If I start with stock 1 full inch thick, I end up with staves about ¾ inch thick. With that knowledge I draw the inside diameter of the container. I will also draw a side view showing the taper, type of hoops to be employed, and handle style. Most of my buckets are about a foot high and use 9 to 12 staves.

For your first try at coopering, select an easily worked wood like pine, basswood, poplar, or Philippine mahogany. Boards 1 inch thick or a bit thicker are ideal and if you have access to a woodpile you may be able to split these out of well-seasoned billets. Cut the staves to length. I suggest making a few extra because they can break while being shaped and sometimes you decide you need an additional one during construction.

Making the concave cut on the inside of each stave is the next step. This grooving out of a perfectly flat board is a rather odd procedure and you may think that special tools are needed, but the good news is that many tools can be used to make this cut and you probably have some of them. For the preliminary rough work I favor an inshave or scorp, but a large gouge, curved adz, carver's hook, or crooked knife would also work. If you insist on using power tools for this step, the board can be passed diagonally over a table-

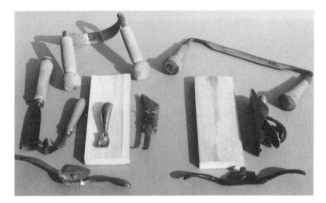

Stave shapers. Tools for making a concave cut at left, those for making convex cut on right.

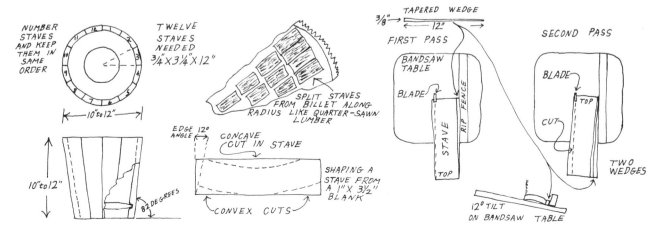

saw blade, or a router or wood hog might be tried. For the finishing cuts I like a curved spokeshave or a round bottom plane. The convex cut on the outside of the staves is easily done with drawknife, spokeshave, or block plane.

I find the best method of tapering the staves for most cooperage is on a band saw, and by tilting the table to 12 degrees I can cut the edge angle at the same time. The band saw must be set up with a rip fence, and you will need two long, tapered wedges for this operation. The diagram shows how this is done. Two passes through the saw are required and each makes a taper and angle cut. Using these wedges is a bit awkward at first but once you get the hang of it this step becomes simple. On cooperage with a steep taper, I find it simpler to work up a template of the stave shape and cut this on the band saw with the table tilted to the correct angle.

At this point the staves can be circled together for a test fitting. A clever way to hold them in place is with long hose clamps. If you don't have any long enough, try splicing some shorter ones together. Undoubtedly some of the edge angles will need correcting, so mark these while the staves are clamped. I trim the staves by mounting them in a vise and using a jack plane. A real cooper has a giant plane mounted bottom side up and passes the staves over this. A few of the edges may be perfect but you will still want to shave off the band-saw tooth marks. Repeat this clamp-and-trim process until you are satisfied with the joints between the staves. Of course, our buckets do not have to be watertight, but it is still desirable to have things fit snugly.

Making and fitting the bottom is the next consideration for our project. I usually band-saw these from a scrap of 1-inch lumber, and taper both edges with a spokeshave. The groove that accepts the bottom should be 1½ to 2 inches from the base of the staves. This distance provides enough wood for sufficient strength below the groove and also allows the bottom rim to fit low enough to really hold the base of the staves. A professional cooper would use a tool called a croze to make this groove. I made one of these from the two ends of a power hacksaw blade and it works fine, but a sharp ½-inch chisel for the cuts and a ¼-inch chisel to clean out the groove does a very satisfactory job. The drawing indicates how the bottom and groove should look. bottom and groove should look.

Elastic straps or large rubber bands are a good way to hold the staves in place while you check the fit of the bottom. Because these flex, you can press the bottom into the bucket from above without total disassembly. When everything fits tightly, you are ready to glue the staves in place. I use yellow glue and apply it only to the stave edges with the idea that the bottom will be happier if it is allowed to expand and contract in its groove. For cooperage to be left outside, I use totally waterproof resorcinol glue. Hose clamps hold the staves in place until the glue dries. Then I smooth up the outside with a block plane and the inside with a round bottom carving plane and finally a curved scraper.

With a solid bucket in hand we are ready to put on the hoops. Normally two are used but there is no rule that says you can't use three. Any more

TECHNICAL NOTES

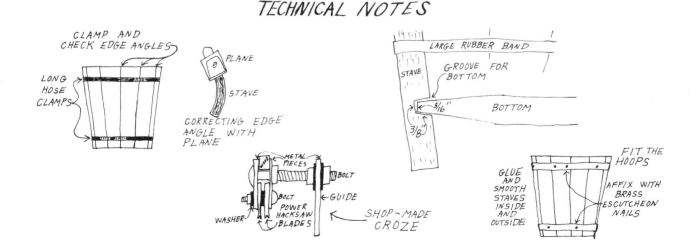

than that and your cooperage will look entirely too "busy." The quickest ones to make are of metal, either recycled from old hoops or fashioned from heavy strap steel of the sort used to hold heavy boxes together. The placement of the hoops is important if the cooperage is to look good. In general, the top hoop should be placed high on the container and the bottom hoop quite low. The following photographs will show this placement. To make metal hoops, cut them to length, drill holes in each end, and rivet them together. Commercial rivets can be used but I often use sawed-off heads from 16-penny nails. Put the hoops in place and check for fit and placement. If the hoops ride too low, the bucket can be planed a bit to slim it down and allow the hoops to ride up. If the hoops need more taper, hammer all around their upper edge on a sturdy steel surface. Too much taper can be corrected by pounding on the lower edge of the hoops. Finally, drive the hoops snugly in place taking care that they are horizontal. Drill tiny holes through the hoops and fasten them to alternate staves with brass escutcheon nails. Wooden hoops and the various types of handles are covered under the individual coopering projects.

I do not sand my cooperage, preferring to have an occasional tool mark show its handmade origin. Also, I often apply no finish to my buckets. If I do apply any finish it is usually only one thin coat, thus allowing the character of the wood and the unusual woodworking to show through.

Making cooperage may not be everyone's bucket of buttermilk, but I feel compelled to urge you to give it a try. If you like it, you may join that rare breed of woodworkers fashioning these unique containers.

PROJECTS

Milk Piggin

With the exception of its one long stave that serves as a handle, a piggin is made like any other piece of cooperage. In bygone times it was used as a giant ladle to transfer milk or other liquids between containers or to hang milk out of harm's way in a barn. Nowadays piggins of all sizes are hung in the garden or patio to hold potted plants, or in the home as containers for dried flower arrangements, keys, letters, tennis balls, or myriad sundry items.

Milk Piggin with sucker hoops and heart decoration.

This Milk Piggin is made somewhat differently from the example in the technical notes. First, it has a slightly oval shape rather than being traditionally rounded. The edge angles must be adjusted to give the container this shape and, of course, the bottom is made oval rather than circular. Second, the hoops are made from split suckers. Usually these are of willow, but any flexible wood will do. I made mine from apricot

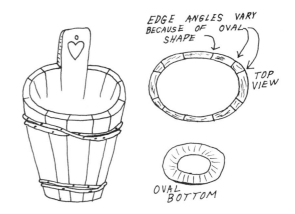

Long hose clamps being used for test-fitting of Milk Piggin. Note that staves are numbered at top.

After gluing staves together, the piggin can be smoothed both inside and out. A spoon-bottom carving plane is in use here.

Firkin

suckers. Shape the suckers as shown and steam for an hour if they lack flexibility. Then wrap the suckers around the piggin and tie them in place until dry. After that, it's an easy matter to drill holes in the suckers and tack them in place with the ends tucked under.

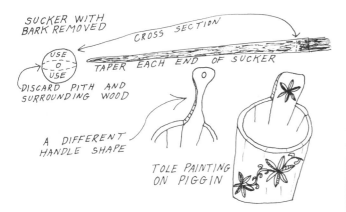

The reverse taper of a firkin gives it a unique place in the lineup of cooperage. I find this shape very pleasing to the eye and it is also a strong and practical form. The modern firkin can be used to hold kindling beside the fireplace, umbrellas or canes beside the front door, or fruit or rolls at a cookout. Because of its crossbar handle, it will not hold a potted plant but it could be used for a

The decoration is a simple heart design carved into the handle and painted blue. The front of the staves could have been painted with tole designs as well. I finished this piece of cooperage with one thin coat of exterior spar varnish.

Using a block plane to smooth the outside of a Firkin.

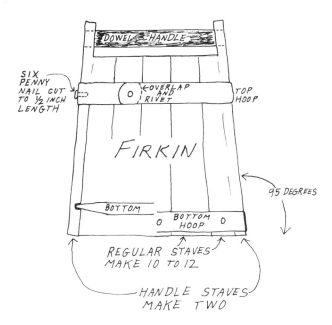

dried arrangement. Its pinched-in top made it valuable for carrying liquids long ago. It is still an official unit of measure, being equal to one fourth of a British barrel.

This Firkin project is constructed of sugar pine and utilizes 10 normal staves and 2 longer handle staves. Remember throughout the construction that the narrow ends of the staves point towards the top. The hoops were recycled from old kegs cut to size and reriveted. They are held in place with 6-penny nails cut to a length of ½ inch. The handle is a length of beechwood dowel that is glued to the handle staves and then rasped flush. I finished this piece of cooperage with one coat of brushing lacquer.

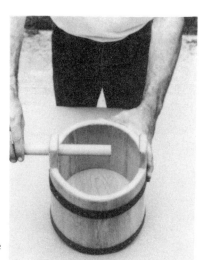

Inserting the handle on a Firkin.

Fruit Bowl

As far as I know, this design is not an ancient example of the cooper's art but rather a recent development. I first saw these on a trip to the southern Appalachian mountains where they were sold to hold fruit, popcorn, chips, or a potted plant. The extreme flare of the sides along with the undulating rim give this container a truly handsome form.

Half of the staves and the bottom for a coopered Fruit Bowl.

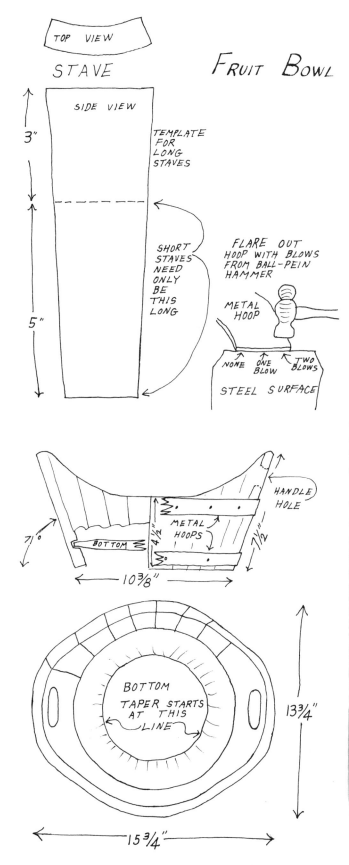

TOP VIEW

STAVE   FRUIT BOWL

SIDE VIEW

3"

TEMPLATE
FOR
LONG
STAVES

SHORT
STAVES
NEED
ONLY
BE
THIS
LONG

FLARE OUT
HOOP WITH BLOWS
FROM BALL-PEIN
HAMMER

METAL
HOOP

5"

NONE ONE TWO
      BLOW BLOWS

STEEL SURFACE

HANDLE
HOLE

METAL
HOOPS

7½"

7|°

BOTTOM

4½"

10⅜"

BOTTOM

TAPER STARTS
AT THIS
LINE

13¾"

15¾"

Because of the greater taper on these staves, I did not try to saw them with my usual wedge spacers. Instead, I worked up a template and cut them freehand with the bandsaw table set at 10 degrees. You will need about 20 staves varying in length from 5 to 8 inches. Plane the edge angle, check for a snug fit, and craft a bottom as for any cooperage project. Because this container is so shallow, I placed the bottom only 1 inch from the base of the staves. This demands that you be careful when chiselling the groove for the bottom.

As the sides on this bowl flare out at an angle of roughly 20 degrees, you will have to flare out the hoops to match this angle. This can be accomplished as described in the technical notes by striking the hoop on its upper edge with the flat face of a ball peen hammer. When everything fits nicely, glue the staves together. The hoops can be clamped on to hold the staves in place while drying. The hoops are anchored to the bowl with escutcheon nails.

Sawing the curved rim and handle holes with a coping saw really brings this project to life. From any side it is a thing of beauty and each time you see the Fruit Bowl you will notice subtle differences in the grain pattern or the shape of the handles. Because I planned to use this bowl to hold food, I sanded the rim smooth and gave the entire container a coat of salad bowl finish.

Coopered Bucket

Up to the point of fabricating the hoops and handle, this bucket is a very standard piece of cooperage, but be advised not to give the sides too much slant or the hoops will not fit well. I used eight regular staves and two longer handle staves of yellow pine for this project. The wooden hoops are made from flaw-free, quarter-sawn white oak. The best way I have found to make these is on a table

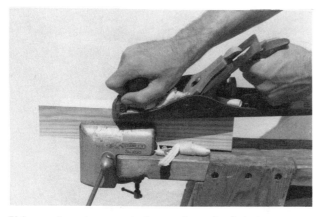

Using a plane to correct edge angle on bucket stave.

saw with a thin kerf, carbide-tipped blade. The hoops are then shaped as shown in the drawing. This is delicate woodworking so proceed slowly and carefully with sharp backsaw, chisels, coping saw, pocket knife, and spokeshave. The locking arrangement on the hoops may look complicated but it is probably the simplest setup that will do the job.

Once made, the hoops must be steamed until flexible. Before forming into a circle, it's a good idea to flex the entire hoop in your hands, but it's especially important to flex the ends of the hoop in an open vise as shown in the drawing, being careful of the weak points. The male end is then twisted, passed through the slot in the female end, and locked in place. If a hoop fits too loosely, a tiny piece of wood can be inserted where the ends lock. If a hoop needs to be longer, a bit of wood can be cut away at the locking point. Fit the hoops horizontally on the bucket and tack into place.

These handles are made from three pieces of steamed and laminated wood. I used white oak

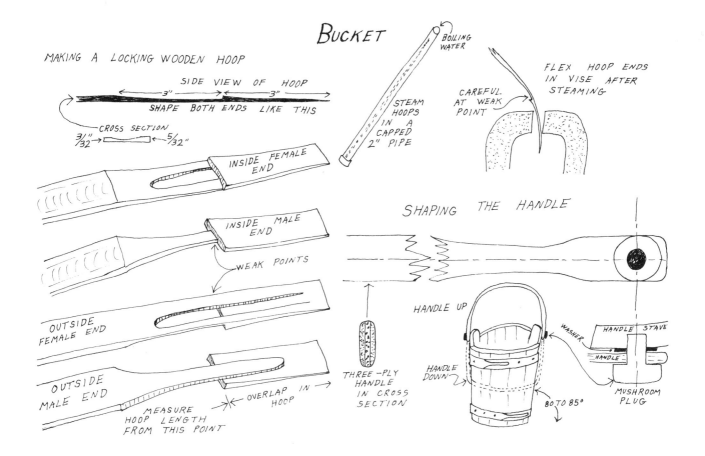

After bottom groove has been cut with chisels or shop-made cruze, to facilitate fitting of bottom the staves are held in place with large rubber bands.

Outside of interlocking hoop. To connect hoop, the male end (*top*) is twisted 90 degrees and passed through the opening in the female end (*bottom*).

and holly on this project. Steam the three plies, bend, and clamp in the proper shape until dry. Then apply yellow glue and clamp again. You can simply round the edges of the handle but I like to sculpt mine as shown in the diagram. The length of my handle is calculated so it will come to rest between the two hoops when folded down. The handle is attached to the long staves with mushroom-shaped pins that you turn or whittle. I usually do not apply any finish to my buckets.

A well-made Coopered Bucket is such a charming product that its uses around the home are well-nigh uncountable. It can serve most of the functions mentioned for the other cooperage projects and lends itself to many others as well. Buckets make great wastebaskets, depositories for knitting or other craft supplies, a clever place to store potholders or other items in a country-style kitchen, and a different way to show off collectibles from teddy bears to glass fish floats.

BASKETS

There are many reasons for getting involved in basket making. It is an enjoyable craft that bestows a wonderful feeling of accomplishment when you handcraft a thing of beauty and utility. It's what I call a "light" craft, in that strength is not required to saw or plane large boards so almost anyone is assured of success. No workshop and few tools are required. In fact, it is possible to get started with just a pocket knife, but craft shears, an awl, and a drill are desirable. Demanding woodworking skills, like the ability to construct tight glue joints, are not needed in basket making. Also it is a clean craft that can be carried on in your living quarters. I often work on baskets in the evening while watching television. So for any or all of these reasons, I hope you will add basket making to your repertoire of skills.

All of our ancestors at one time belonged to a hunting-gathering society and these groups needed containers to hold their daily collection of fish, clams, nuts, or roots. In most cases, these containers were baskets, and some of these groups developed this craft to a fine degree, making baskets for gathering, storing, winnowing, sifting, leaching, water carrying, and cooking. You may challenge my statement that aborigines could carry liquids or do their cooking in baskets, but it's true. Both types of baskets were finely and tightly woven. The ones for carrying water were usually coated with melted resin on the inside, while the ones for cooking were filled with water and ground roots, nuts, or seeds, and heated by dropping in hot rocks. The cooked gruel filled any holes in the basket. When these primitive groups took up agriculture, they settled into villages and learned to make pottery. As pottery stands up to the aeons better than basketry, we know much more about ancient pots than we do baskets, but museums still have plenty of stunning examples to inspire the modern basket maker.

I made my first basket many years ago to pass the test for a Boy Scout merit badge and have maintained an interest in this fascinating craft ever since. As a woodworker I find many differences in basket making but also many similarities, especially in the materials used which include white oak, ash, and the same cane that is used in making rattan furniture and chair seats. For me basketry is not an exact science. The flexibility of the material precludes precise measurements and complete conformity. Rather than being concerned about this, I use it to my advantage by making baskets to relax, so I don't worry about whether a piece is exactly round or whether every end is tucked in precisely the same.

The simplest definition I can come up with for a basket is that it is a bunch of flexible "stuff" that is woven, coiled, or twined together to form some sort of container. Nomenclature for baskets is only vaguely standardized. A few distinctive types, like the key, potato, and hen baskets, seem to retain the identical name everywhere. By and large, however, the naming of baskets is rather an

Baskets shown left to right: (*top*) Potato Basket, Ribbed Basket of oak splits, Straight-Sided Basket; (*bottom*) Hen Basket of binder cane, Island Basket using a Cherokee pattern, and a straight-sided Magazine Basket of oak.

A Key Basket (*left*) incorporates two colors of dyed flat cane and another has weavers of binder cane and grass rope (*center*). The Island Basket (*right*) has a drawstring top and shoulder strap to be used as a purse.

individual affair. You will find a style called a harvest basket in one area called a vegetable basket in another.

Baskets were of vital importance to ancient societies and they remain important today. They still perform well as wastebaskets, laundry hampers, picnic baskets, and as the ideal container for collecting flowers, vegetables, and fruits from the garden. For strength, beauty, and usefulness, a basket is hard to beat.

TECHNICAL NOTES

Basketry Materials

So many materials are used worldwide for basket making that I will only cover the most important of them. Native basket makers in North America used willow, honeysuckle and blackberry stems, spruce roots, agave and yucca leaves, the inner bark of hickory, poplar and cedar trees, a number of swamp and prairie grasses, and pine needles for making baskets. In the tropics, rattan cane, bamboo, raffia, sisal, and jute fiber were widely used. Two special plants were utilized in the Orient. They are usually referred to as Chinese grass and Japanese mat grass. On the Pacific islands, pandanus leaves from the screw pine tree and the mid-ribs of coconut palms are favorite basket materials. Eskimos and other people from the far north had few plants to use for basket making but they did have baleen from toothless whales. Two woody plants, much used for basketry in the New World, are white oak and black ash. The stems of cereal grains are utilized for the construction of coiled baskets throughout the world. Birch bark is one of the most unusual basket-making materials. It was used in Northern Europe and the skill was brought to Canada and the United States by Scandinavian immigrants.

The material for making baskets emanates almost entirely from the plant kingdom, but it does not arrive from nature ready for use. Willow twigs, for example, are debarked for most baskets, but if they are to be used for wrapping they are split into quarters and scraped thin. Rattan cane is cut into several shapes, the two most popular being flat and round, but it is also available in a flattened oval shape. Rattan cane that is cut from the edge of a stem is called binder cane. The cane used for chair and canoe seats is a thin version of this. Yucca leaves can be used for some jobs by simply splitting them, but agave and

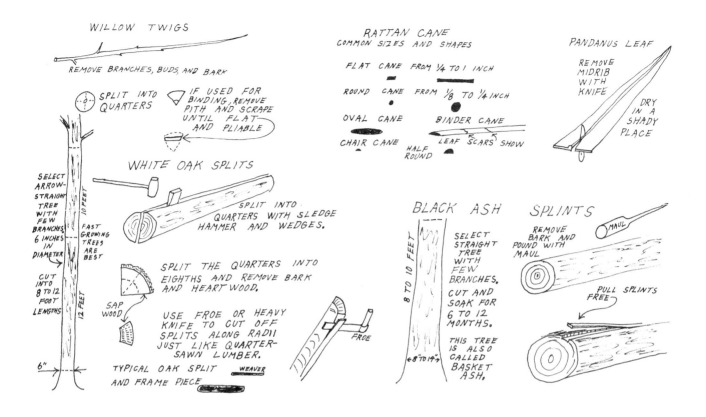

PREPARATION AND SIZE OF BASKET—MAKING MATERIAL

WILLOW TWIGS

REMOVE BRANCHES, BUDS, AND BARK

SPLIT INTO QUARTERS

IF USED FOR BINDING, REMOVE PITH AND SCRAPE UNTIL FLAT AND PLIABLE

RATTAN CANE
COMMON SIZES AND SHAPES

FLAT CANE FROM 1/4 TO 1 INCH

ROUND CANE FROM 1/8 TO 1/4 INCH

OVAL CANE   BINDER CANE

CHAIR CANE   HALF ROUND   LEAF SCARS SHOW

PANDANUS LEAF

REMOVE MIDRIB WITH KNIFE

DRY IN A SHADY PLACE

WHITE OAK SPLITS

SELECT ARROW-STRAIGHT TREE WITH FEW BRANCHES 6 INCHES IN DIAMETER

FAST GROWING TREES ARE BEST

CUT INTO 8 TO 12 FOOT LENGTHS

10 FEET

12 FEET

6"

SPLIT INTO QUARTERS WITH SLEDGE HAMMER AND WEDGES.

SPLIT THE QUARTERS INTO EIGHTHS AND REMOVE BARK AND HEARTWOOD.

SAP WOOD

USE FROE OR HEAVY KNIFE TO CUT OFF SPLITS ALONG RADII JUST LIKE QUARTER-SAWN LUMBER.

FROE

TYPICAL OAK SPLIT AND FRAME PIECE   WEAVER

BLACK ASH   SPLINTS

SELECT STRAIGHT TREE WITH FEW BRANCHES. CUT AND SOAK FOR 6 TO 12 MONTHS. THIS TREE IS ALSO CALLED BASKET ASH.

8 TO 10 FEET

8" TO 14"

REMOVE BARK AND POUND WITH MAUL

MAUL

PULL SPLINTS FREE

most of the bark fibers must be separated from the surrounding plant tissue before use. Pandanus leaves are split to remove the midrib and allowed to season before they are ready for weaving. Rye is the strongest of the cereal grain stems. For basket use it should be cut close to the ground before harvesting and hung in a shady spot. When dry the grain and leaves are removed. Handle the other grains in a similar manner. Pine needles and birch bark can be used green, or after soaking in water if they are dry.

White oak splits and black ash splints are available for the labor to anyone who has access to suitable logs, otherwise they can be purchased. They are both light and strong and make great baskets but let me warn you they do involve considerable sweat and perhaps some splinters as well. White oak splits are made from fast-growing, arrow-straight saplings not over 6 inches at the base. These are usually found growing in a clump in a moist spot. All of the trees in the clump will not live to maturity, so you are following sound forestry practice by thinning one out.

Cutting oak splits with a heavy knife.

An average tree will yield two logs from 8 to 12 feet in length. These logs are quartered with wedges and a sledge hammer, and the heartwood split away. The bark is removed from the sap wood which is worked into long splits with froe and sheath knife. Heavy leather gloves will prevent splinters. Oak logs are best worked when green. If the splits dry out they can be made flexible again by soaking. Ash splints are made by cutting logs 8 to 14 inches in diameter and throwing them in a pond for six to twelve months. They are pulled out and pounded with a wooden

The evolution of ribs for an Island Basket starting with billets sawn to length on the left and ending with finished ribs on the right.

Frames

Any wood that can be steamed and bent can be used for basket frames. (See information on wood bending in the introductory chapter.) I make most of my frames from white oak about ⅛ inch thick, either cut on the table saw or hand-split from sapwood. If a sharp bend is called for in the frame, I will thin the wood a bit at that point. Sometimes it is necessary to double the frame for sufficient strength at the corners or for a handle. Before bending, the frame is soaked in hot water or steamed. For some basket designs it's desirable to make a jig. The steamed frame pieces are bent around the jig and clamped in place until dry.

I employ two methods to hold the frames together. The most permanent of these, and my favorite, is brass escutcheon nails. Be sure to drill holes in the frame for these. The 1 inch length can be cut to size and mushroomed over like a rivet while the ¾ inch ones can be used full-length and bent over. However, only do this if the bent-over point is to be covered with binding. The other method I use is to tie the frame members together. This method can fail in time so it is very important to use strong material for tying. At var-

maul to loosen the splints, which are actually the annual rings.

Basket-making material must be soaked in water before use. Splits and splints may have to be soaked for an hour or so, but rattan cane is normally ready for use in 15 minutes, and fine stuff like raffia may only have to be submerged a few seconds. Don't use hot water, but I find that warm water speeds up the soaking process on coarse stuff. I suggest not leaving any weaving material in water overnight as mildew may discolor it.

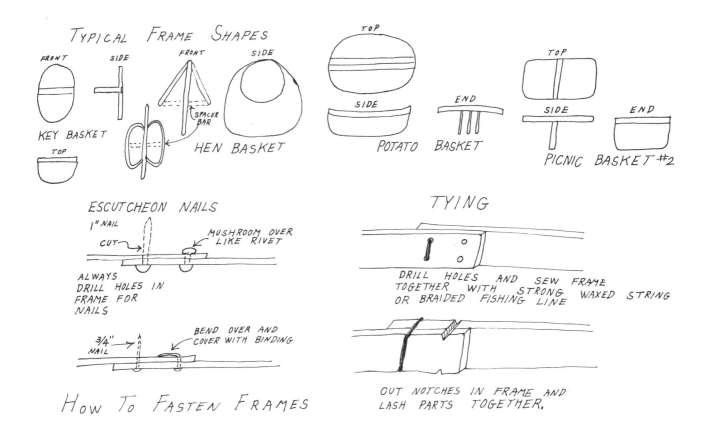

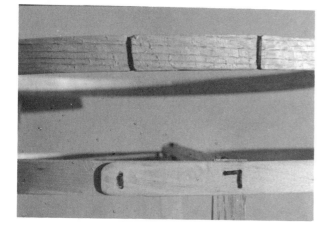

Two ways to tie basket frames: with notches (*at the top*), and with holes (*below*).

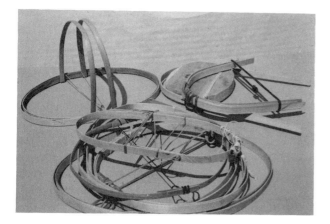

A collection of basket frame members and handles that have been bent and tied into shape after steaming.

ious times I have used linen or nylon string or braided fishing line. This material should be well waxed and can be threaded through small holes in the frame or around notches. Ideally the line for tying should be the same color as your basket material.

Types of Baskets

There are many styles of baskets and no book can hope to cover them all but I have attempted to include a wide selection. One of the simplest styles has a flat straight-sided bottom made with a basic over and under weave. The pieces used to form the bottom are turned up to form the sides and held in place with a weaver. A rim and perhaps a handle completes this project. Any piece of basket-making material that passes between standing parts, ribs, or spokes is called a weaver. Weavers are normally the longest pieces you have.

When you come to the end of a weaver, overlap a new piece 4 to 8 inches and continue to work. The tag ends of the weavers are best hidden at an inconspicuous spot on the inside of the basket.

When a weaver goes around a basket with an odd number of members in a basic over and under weave, it "works" and you can continue weaving for several rows. If you have an even number of members you must take some action because your second and third row will be exactly like the first and your basket will not hold together. In my language, I would say the weaver "does not work." There are various ways to correct this problem. The easiest way is to split one of the members, thus producing an odd number. Or, you can incorporate an additional spoke or rib to form an uneven number. Another method involves going over or under two of the standing members. Although this does not change the number of members it changes the number you weave around and you discover that your weaver now works. You can continue this technique as you weave by moving over one member each time before going over or under two. A fourth method is available, but I hardly ever use it because I think it results in a weaker basket. In this method, instead of utilizing a continuous weaver, a new piece of weaver is used for each row. If you use this system be sure to rotate the basket so that all the joints are not on the same side. On some baskets new ribs are added a number of times. This will sometimes result in an even number of ribs. The solution is simple: just pass over or under two ribs to get your weaver back on track. You will notice these intentional "mistakes" on some of the baskets in this chapter.

An oak-split magazine basket under construction.

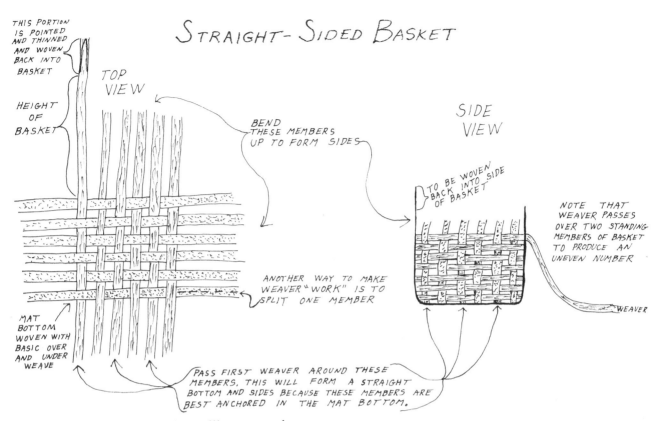

STRAIGHT-SIDED BASKET

TOP VIEW

THIS PORTION IS POINTED AND THINNED AND WOVEN BACK INTO BASKET

HEIGHT OF BASKET

BEND THESE MEMBERS UP TO FORM SIDES

SIDE VIEW

TO BE WOVEN BACK INTO SIDE OF BASKET

NOTE THAT WEAVER PASSES OVER TWO STANDING MEMBERS OF BASKET TO PRODUCE AN UNEVEN NUMBER

ANOTHER WAY TO MAKE WEAVER "WORK" IS TO SPLIT ONE MEMBER

WEAVER

MAT BOTTOM WOVEN WITH BASIC OVER AND UNDER WEAVE

PASS FIRST WEAVER AROUND THESE MEMBERS, THIS WILL FORM A STRAIGHT BOTTOM AND SIDES BECAUSE THESE MEMBERS ARE BEST ANCHORED IN THE MAT BOTTOM.

Another easily made basket utilizes a number of spokes that can be either flat or round to form a bottom. A weaver is used to hold the spokes in place on the bottom and continues this function when they are bent up to form the sides. When the basket is tall enough, the spokes are bent back on themselves and woven into the body of the basket. This basket is usually finished with a rim and handle.

The majority of baskets in this chapter are made with ribs. Ribbed baskets come in many handsome, functional styles and are fun to make. These ribs are anchored in place initially by the

ROUND-BOTTOM SPOKED BASKET

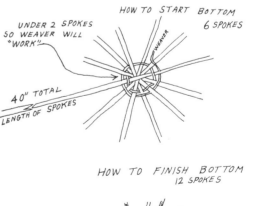

HOW TO START BOTTOM 6 SPOKES

UNDER 2 SPOKES SO WEAVER WILL "WORK"

WEAVER

40" TOTAL LENGTH OF SPOKES

HOW TO FINISH BOTTOM 12 SPOKES

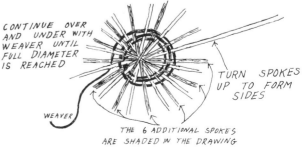

CONTINUE OVER AND UNDER WITH WEAVER UNTIL FULL DIAMETER IS REACHED

TURN SPOKES UP TO FORM SIDES

WEAVER

THE 6 ADDITIONAL SPOKES ARE SHADED IN THE DRAWING

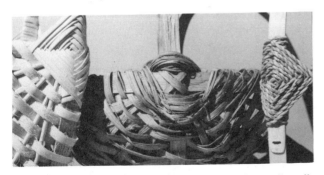

A good way to start ribbed baskets is to make an "eye." Three are shown here, made (*left to right*) with ¼-inch flat cane, oak split, and grass rope.

binding that goes around the junction of the frame and handle. This binding, which reminds me of the "Eye of God" used in the art of the Southwest, is commonly referred to as an eye. To anchor the first ribs in this eye, and subsequent ribs into the weaving, it is necessary to whittle a long slender point on each end. Once in place, a rib becomes part of the basket's skeleton. The weavers pass over and under it as well as the frame. Additional ribs are used when needed. If you skimp on ribs you will end up with a weak basket.

Handles and Rims

Handles and rims perform an important function on baskets and should be made both strong and graceful. Some handles are built right into the basket, as with the hen and potato styles. On others, you can select the handle you like. Three of the most common types are a folding handle, similar to a bail on a bucket, a fixed handle of the same type, and baskets with two small handles on either side. The latter type can be carried against the chest by a single person or by two people walking side by side.

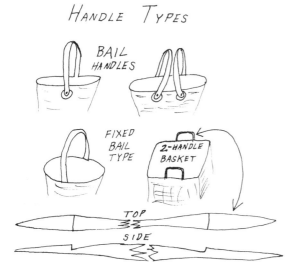

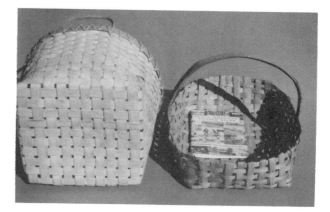

Two Straight-Sided Baskets showing different handles.

On ribbed baskets, the rim is usually part of the original frame and is more or less covered with weaving. On many other baskets the rim is added when the basket sides have reached the height you desire. The finishing touch on rims can be a simple wraparound with binder cane or strips of leather, or a fancier design with loops and such.

Basket Strength

One of the many nice things about baskets is that they don't break. If you drop a china bowl on a concrete patio it will shatter because it is brittle. A metal pot won't shatter but might dent because it's malleable. But a dropped basket will bounce and lay there none the worse for the fall. Naturally, this is because the basket is made of material that is both tough and flexible. This is rather like the pliant side of a kayak bouncing off a rock in white water whereas the side of a rigidly constructed boat might be stove in.

Basket Decoration

I decorate my baskets in four ways. One is by using different textures of materials. For example, I might use grass rope or binder cane for the eye and the initial tight weaving, and then switch to rattan cane or oak splits for the more open areas. My second method is simply to vary the size of the weavers I use to form a pattern. The third is to weave a design into the basket by going over two and under two to form a sort of herringbone, or other similar pattern. The fourth way is by incorporating dyed material. To add color to the baskets in this chapter I used two types of home-

Picnic Basket #2 showing the transition from binder-cane to flat-cane weaver.

made dye. A dark brown dye was produced by simmering two quarts of black walnut hulls in a like amount of water for about 30 minutes, then straining. A light orange dye was made by soaking padauk shavings in acetone for 15 minutes. To dye rattan cane, immerse it in either of these strained liquids for five minutes or until it is as dark as you desire. Oak and ash can be dyed but the results are less satisfactory. When dry, the cane is ready to use, but be aware that the black walnut dye is water-soluble so if you have to soak this material before use you may lose some of the intensity of the color. The easy way around this is to use it as soon as you remove it from the dye. Also, be careful about this dye bleeding onto uncolored portions of your basket.

Of course, permanent commercial dyes can be used, but as a dyed-in-the-wool woodworker I prefer to produce my own colors from forest products. Many other things can be used to decorate baskets, from colored fibres and feathers to beads and seashells. There is nothing wrong with doing this. Various native-made baskets from around the world employ such decorations. However, I use such material sparingly for the simple reason that I like the graceful lines of the basket to show through without too much tinsel detracting.

Reshaping

Occasionally you will notice that a completed basket sits a bit to one side or has an unsightly bulge. I use three methods to correct uneven bottoms and the last of these can be employed on bulges. One method I call the doughnut technique

is nothing more than affixing a circle of weaver material around the bottom. A similar method that works well on oak-split baskets is weaving rails or skids with flexible ends into the bottom of the basket. My last system involves soaking the bottom, or any other abnormal, bulging area of the basket, and reshaping it. A saucer and a round pan help do the reshaping on the bottom. For other areas you will have to devise clamps and braces that will bend your basket back to its proper shape. The drawing shows these three methods.

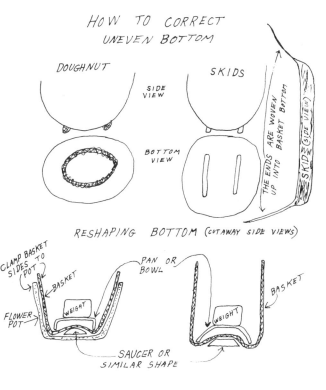

A stabilizing doughnut on the bottom of an oak-split basket.

Construction Tips

The following are tidbits of information that I have found useful in basket making:

1. Always try to have the best face of the material on the outside of the basket. The best side will be smooth and uniform while the other side may have splinters, whiskers, stains, or other flaws.

2. Occasionally you will come across a very weak piece of basket-making material. Toss it in the fireplace so it won't break during construction or contribute to a fragile basket.

3. If you must make a sharp bend in a piece of material already in a basket be sure to resoak it first. Then flex it between your fingers several times before bending. If it still resists bending, thin it down with a knife or scraper and soak and flex again.

4. An awl is a handy tool when inserting ribs into an eye or into existing weaving on a basket. First insert the awl and then push the pointed rib in beside it.

5. Small spring clamps are useful for holding basket parts in place. This is especially true when you are just starting a project and it seems that five hands are required. Spring clothespins will suffice on light work.

6. Many basket-making materials, but especially rattan cane, shrink when they dry. The small amount they shrink in length is of no consequence, but their loss of width makes for a loose basket. To solve this, weave tightly as you proceed but don't get carried away or you may pull your project out of shape. When you have completed the weaving, lay the basket aside without cutting off the weaver. Inspect the work in a day or two to ascertain the amount of shrinkage. If the basket is loose, just continue with the weaver to tighten up the work.

7. Many ribbed baskets have odd shapes, so when you are weaving back and forth between frame members you may cover all of the perimeter of the rim before the basket is completed. Just continue to weave between the remaining ribs in as neat a manner as possible until the basket is finished.

8. Sometimes when I'm working on a basket I'll discover that a rib or rim is too weak. If not corrected this could result in a warped basket. My answer to this problem is to insert a

On your lap, a comfortable position for working on baskets.

shorter section of rib or rim next to the original. In extreme cases I may add more than one piece.

9. If you feel you are "all thumbs" on your first attempt at basket making, don't despair. Your dexterity is sure to improve with practice. You may also find it difficult to discover a comfortable working position while weaving. One of my favorites is to sit with the basket in my lap. At other times I place the basket on a table and sit in front of it. Occasionally I straddle a bench with the basket on the bench in front of me.

10. If you have occasion to split flat cane splits or splints, do it with a craft shears or hefty scissors. If you try to do it with a knife, your cut will almost certainly run out the side.

11. On a few baskets you will find that spreaders are needed to keep the basket in its proper shape during construction. I make these from shop scrap, often using two pieces nailed together so that I can take them apart for removal should they become totally trapped within the basket.

12. When you are working with a weaver it is almost always easier to pass it around the ends of the standing parts of the basket than to thread the weaver between these parts. If you get both hands involved, with one separating the spokes and the other passing the weaver through, you can work quite efficiently. On most ribbed baskets you must thread the weaver through because both ends of the ribs are anchored in place.

13. When I finish the construction of a basket, I give it sort of a haircut. With craft shears, I trim off all the whiskers that have formed during weaving as well as cut off any tag ends of weavers.

14. If one of my baskets is to receive hard outdoor use, like the packbasket, I give it two coats of spar urethane. On all others, I like the natural feel of the materials to come through.

As you look over these basketry projects, you will notice that I use leather in a number of my baskets. I like to work with leather and I think it marries well with oak, ash, and cane, but I need no justification because I believe in people developing their own individual styles. To that end, I urge you to try variations on these themes to make baskets that are uniquely yours.

PROJECTS

Straight-Sided Basket

This is a good first project. It has straightforward construction, is easy to start, and lends itself to variations in size, height, and type of handle. The square basket is made of rattan cane and makes a fine harvest basket, a container for knitting or craft supplies, or an all-around container. The rectangular model is constructed of oak splits and is an ideal shape for storing magazines.

Commence this basket by weaving a mat of flat cane the size and shape of the basket you desire. I used ¾-inch cane for this. The pieces of cane protruding from this mat are then bent vertical to form the sides. This results in an even number of standing members, so I split one thus allowing my weaver to work. At the base I used ¾-inch cane for my weaver. About halfway up the side, I incorporated one weaver of 1 inch width and finished the weaving with ½-inch cane. The standing members are thinned, pointed, folded back on themselves, and woven into the basket. The handles were carved, steamed and bent, and inserted into the top of the basket. An inner and outer rim was bent around the basket and lashed in place with two rows of ¼-inch binder cane in a chevron design. The drawings in the technical notes cover the details of this basket's construction.

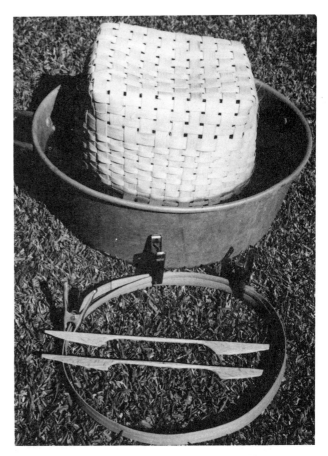

Soaking the standing members of a Straight-Sided Basket before weaving them back into basket. Rim and handles below.

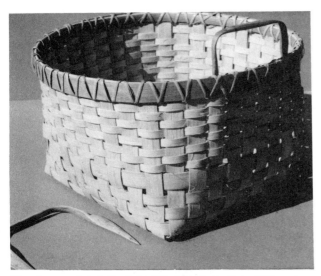

Nearly completed Straight-Sided Basket. Note different thickness of weavers and "V" design on rim.

Round-Bottom Basket

This, like the first project, is a basic basket with many uses that lends itself to many variations in size, decoration, and handle styles. It is, however, a bit trickier to get started. I first laid out 6 spokes of ¾-inch flat cane, each 40 inches long, and wove a piece of binder cane twice around the 12 ends. Next I laid 6 more spokes over the top of these and continued weaving with the binder cane around all 24 ends. At this point I started using ½-inch flat cane as a weaver. When the bottom reached a diameter of 11 inches, I bent the spokes vertically to form the sides and continued weaving with the flat cane.

To make the weaver work, I skipped two spokes after weaving around the basket once. On the next go-round, I moved over one spoke and again skipped two spokes. This "skip" pattern proceeds around the basket in a diagonal line to the top. This method of making a weaver work

A Round-Bottom Basket showing first six spokes held together with binder-cane weaver.

The same basket with six more spokes placed on top. Note the weaver passing over two spokes to make it "work."

This almost finished Round-Bottom Basket has the rim and handle in place. The standing members are being bent over the rim and woven back into the sides.

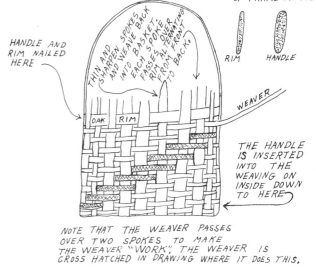

strengthens as well as adds a touch of decoration to the basket. When the basket reached 9 inches in height, I added a rim and inserted a fixed bail handle. The handle and rim are attached with brass nails that were cut off and mushroomed over. Each spoke end was thinned, pointed, and woven back into the basket.

Ribbed Basket

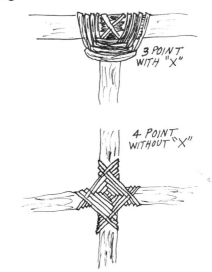

EYES

3 POINT WITH "X"

4 POINT WITHOUT "X"

This is the first of a number of Ribbed Baskets presented in this section. Instructions for weaving are given in greater detail in the technical notes of this section. The oak frame consists of a rim and handle that can be nailed or tied together. The dimensions are roughly 18 by 18 by 15 inches high. I started by making eyes of grass rope at both rim–handle junctions and continued using this material as a weaver. Very quickly, I introduced two oak ribs on each side. After some additional weaving, I added three more ribs on each side

making a total of 10 ribs plus two rim members and the handle base for a total of 13. This being a nice odd number, my weaver worked beautifully. Once I reached a less curvaceous area I switched to long, thin oak splits for weavers. Because the bottom of the basket is rounded, you will probably want to stabilize it. I did this with two skids.

This basket was made many years ago and was one of my first attempts at working with oak splits. It's a bit primitive but has a certain rugged charm. The basket's held up well through years of use as a depository for paperback books.

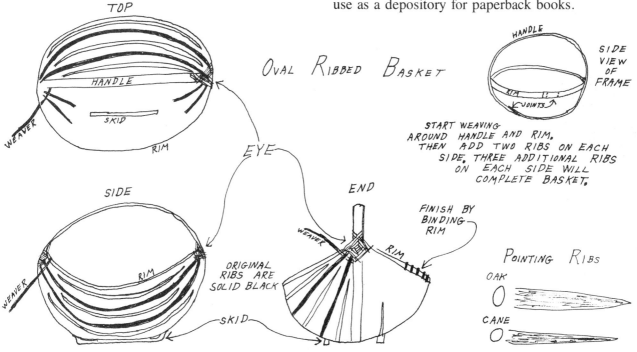

TOP

HANDLE

WEAVER

SKID

RIM

OVAL RIBBED BASKET

SIDE

WEAVER

RIM

EYE

SIDE VIEW OF FRAME

HANDLE

RIM

JOINTS

START WEAVING AROUND HANDLE AND RIM. THEN ADD TWO RIBS ON EACH SIDE. THREE ADDITIONAL RIBS ON EACH SIDE WILL COMPLETE BASKET.

END

WEAVER

ORIGINAL RIBS ARE SOLID BLACK

SKID

FINISH BY BINDING RIM

RIM

POINTING RIBS

OAK

CANE

Potato Basket

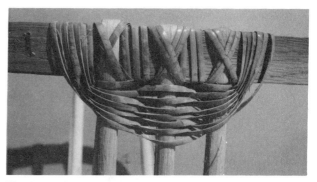

The start of a Potato Basket showing the oak rim and three permanent ribs lashed in place with binder cane.

This is not an elegant basket but rather a serviceable design that produces a strong, practical basket of a kind that long ago could be dragged through the fields while harvesting crops. It is the first basket we have seen where the rim becomes the handles. Another difference is that it has three permanent ribs that along with the rim become the frame.

Because the strips of oak I used for the rim were rather light, I used two of them. The traditional Potato Basket has three strong ribs placed perpendicular to the weaving. These are lashed to the rim with their ends sticking up. Those ends struck me as an invitation to splinters, so I made my ribs from oval cane bent clear around the rim and reinforced on the inside.

Once you have bent and tied your rim you are ready to attach the permanent ribs. The drawing shows how I did this. I lashed the ribs in place with thin binder cane and continued weaving around the ribs and the rim with this material. Next, I added three ribs on each side and switched to ¼-inch binder cane. I proceeded to weave with the binder cane, then added two more ribs on each side, and eventually started using ½-inch flat cane as a weaver. When this weaving was within 5 inches of meeting in the middle I dropped my weaving down to the top rib. I beefed up this rib with two sections of round cane. I also strengthened the portion of rim that was to become the handle before wrapping it with leather. The example shown in the photos is about 17 by 19 by 8 inches in size.

Two-Rimmed Basket

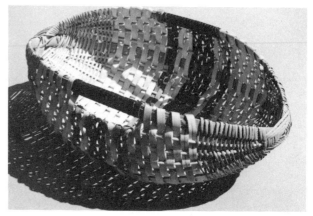

This looks somewhat like a Potato Basket but it is made quite differently. Depending on the angle at which the two rims are crossed, this design can

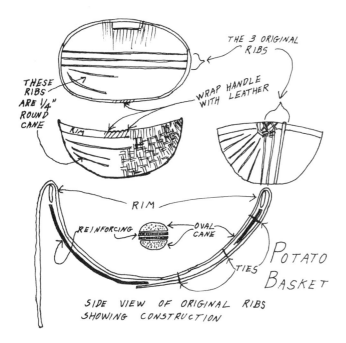

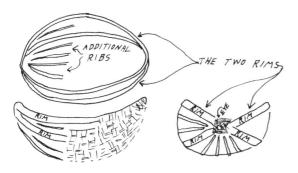

Two-Rimmed Basket

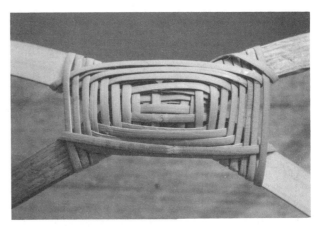

Close-up of rectangular eye used on Two-Rimmed Basket.

show a lot of flair. If your rims are elliptical, like mine, your basket will take on a football shape, but it can be made with round rims as well. I used ¼-inch round cane for the ribs.

Start by making two rims of the same size, shape, and strength. These are lashed in place, at both ends, with strong cord. Next, take any sort of light weaver and make an eye over this lashing. Your eye will probably turn out to be a rectangle because of the acute angle at which the rims are crossed. Insert ribs into the eye to form a bottom and between the rims to form sides. Start weaving around these ribs and the rims. The first few turns may seem a bit odd because of the rectangular shape of the eye, but the weaving will even out after a few turns. Work in more ribs as needed.

As with the previous basket project, the weavers for the Two-Rimmed Basket drop to the ribs below the rim to form the handles. To add color, I worked some dyed flat cane into the center of this project. Finish the handles by wrapping with leather, grass rope, or binder cane.

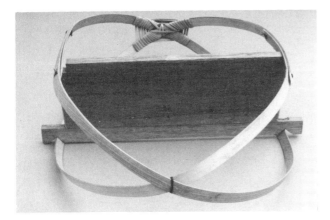

The frame of a Two-Rimmed Basket showing one eye completed and the wood spacer used at the start of weaving.

Key Basket

These half baskets, which are designed to hang on a wall, were probably used as a depository for the large keys that were common years ago, hence their name. Today they are ideal for guest towels in the bathroom, pot holders in the kitchen, letters to be mailed in the office, a dried arrangement anywhere, and, yes, even for keys.

The frame consists of a full oval and a half round. Fasten them together as shown in the frame construction drawings in the Technical Notes. Make a four-point eye where the frame

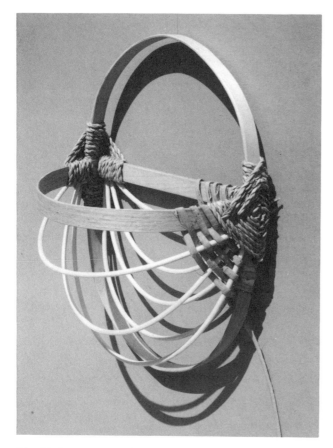

The binder-cane weaving has just started on this Key Basket. Note the grass-rope eyes and the ¼-inch round-cane ribs.

The graceful lines of the Hen Basket make it one of my favorites.

The initial weaving on this Hen Basket shows the two smaller loops of the frame held apart by a wooden spacer. Also notice the leather-wrapped handle and round-cane ribs.

parts meet. The eye will wrap around the back of the frame. This will seem a bit odd but it is quite easy to do. Next, insert three ribs in the front and four in the back. I used ³⁄₁₆-inch cane for this. Start weaving at both eyes and work until your weavers meet in the middle. Different colors and textures have been incorporated into the key baskets shown here.

Hen Basket

With its beautiful curves, to my mind this basket rates as one of the most gorgeous, yet it had humble beginnings having been designed to carry laying fowl. Three sturdy loops are required for the frame. The two smaller ones are the same size and should be about half the diameter of the larger one. See the Hen Basket frame illustration in the Technical Notes. Note that a spacer is used to keep the sides of this project from caving in during construction.

Start by binding 4 inches of the three rings together. I used leather, but binder cane could have been used. The weaving begins with just the three loops, but as soon as the distance between these becomes too great start adding ribs of ¼-inch cane. I used 16 ribs but might have gotten by with only 14. Keep all the bottom ribs the same length so that the basket will tend to have a flat bottom. If your basket does not stand straight, follow the procedures outlined under the Technical Notes. Continue weaving until the basket is completed. As I used binder cane for this entire basket, I had to twist the weaver at the end of each pass to keep the shiny side out.

Doughnut Basket

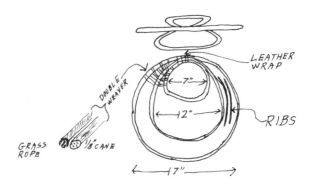

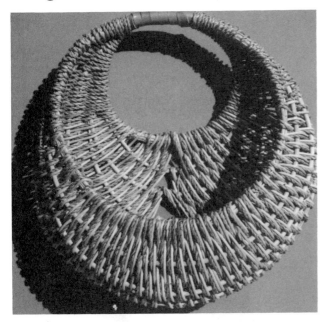

This basket is meant for hanging, much like the key basket, but it is constructed in a manner more suggestive of the Hen Basket. Note that a scrap-wood jig is needed to keep the frame and ribs spread during weaving. I made the three loops for the frame from oval cane and bound the top with leather. The diameters of the loops are 7, 12, and 17 inches. For a weaver I used grass rope and ⅛-inch cane side by side as if they were one piece. This is the first time here that I have used this technique. It not only gives the basket an unusual texture, but the cane weaver provides a great deal of strength and cuts down on the number of ribs needed. Start weaving on both sides of the leather wrap and work until finished.

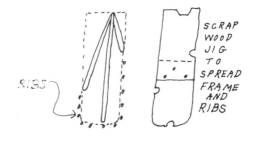

A Doughnut Basket showing the three different-size loops forming the frame and two round-cane ribs. Notice the two-piece wood spacer.

Fishing Basket

I do not call this a creel because I did not set out to duplicate the Korean willow model. As a dedicated trout fisherman, I set up the following criteria for my Fishing Basket:

1. A well-ventilated container, strong enough and water-resistant enough to stand up to rough field use.
2. Large enough to hold 10 trout, some as long as 16 inches.
3. Light weight and conveniently shaped for easy carrying.
4. A lid that is simple to open and close, with a hole in the lid for depositing fish.

I commenced construction by making a frame for the bottom from oval and flat cane. The drawing shows how I made this composite piece. I glued this with waterproof glue and drilled it to accept the upright members that would form the sides. These side members were ⅛-inch round cane, and they also form the ribs for the bottom of the basket. The bottom was woven in with ³⁄₁₆-inch binder cane. Note in the drawing that a second piece of ⅛-inch cane is incorporated next to each of the upright members.

The weaver for the sides is ⅛-inch round cane just like the uprights. The sides consist of nothing but standard weaving until the front reaches the

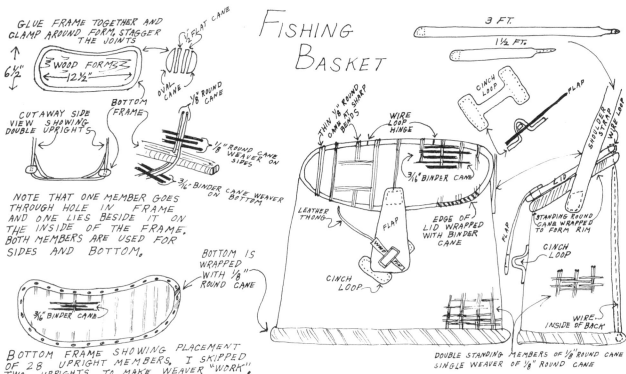

correct height. When I reached that point, I continued weaving to make the back higher so that the lid would fall closed even if I was stumbling around in a fast brook with a lunker on my line. I did this by weaving around the back and then reversing the weave at one of the front uprights. I kept dropping back one upright on each side until I reached the back of the basket. At this point I discontinued weaving because I wanted the back straight and level so I could use it to hinge the lid. The rim of this fishing basket was made strong by wrapping the uprights around the top of the woven sides. As I had double uprights, I first wrapped one set and then the other.

I fashioned the lid frame from ¼-inch round cane with a long, tapered overlap joined with waterproof glue. Next, I measured the top into 1¼-inch segments and wrapped ⅛-inch round cane around these as shown in the sketch. You may have to thin the cane at the sharp bends. When these canes were dry, I wove in the top with ³⁄₁₆-inch binder cane. I placed the hole for inserting trout at one end of the lid and finished the lid by binding its perimeter with binder cane. The top is attached with two loops of stainless-steel wire. These are run down inside the weaving on the back and anchored to the bottom frame. I next gave my fishing basket two coats of spar urethane.

The shoulder strap and lid-closing device are simple leatherwork. I used light cowhide for the strap and medium-weight cowhide for the closure. The leather is first cut to size and then holes are punched in it to accept the heavy waxed thread with which it is sewn. An awl is employed to spread the cane so a needle can be used to stitch the leather parts in place. To fasten the closed lid I used a tapered piece of cherry with a thong glued into its end to prevent loss.

Close-up of the Fishing Basket's closing mechanism.

Picnic Basket #1

This chapter includes three picnic-potluck baskets. The first project covered introduces some different design elements, like a wooden lid and elongated weavers that become a handle. Also there is an optional wood platform inside that makes it possible to carry both a deep and a shallow dish.

I began the basket by bending a sturdy oak rim and the six primary oak ribs as shown in the drawing. I bent the ribs over the rim at each end, creating a nub. These two nubs served later to hold the lid in place. The initial weaving is with

Three types of Picnic Basket: #1 (*upper right*) with wooden lid, #2 (*foreground*) with a double-hinged lid, and #3 (*upper left*) a large Island Basket.

A construction photo of Picnic Basket #1. The materials consist of white-oak splits and grass rope. Note that the handle is formed from three elongated loops of weaver.

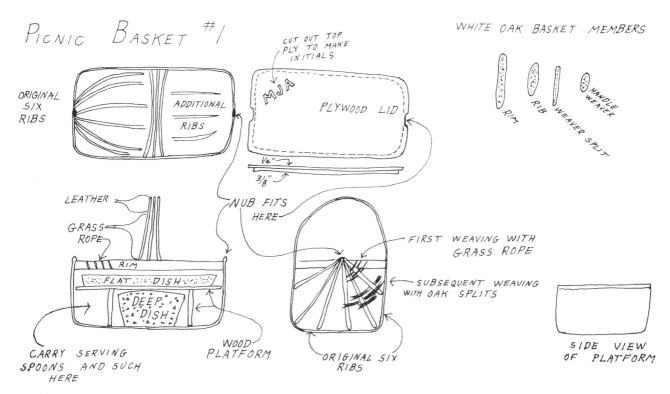

Picnic Basket #1

grass rope. I switched to oak-split weavers and introduced five additional ribs as I proceeded.

When I reached the center of the basket I made sure to use narrow but rather thick weavers to assure that the handle had sufficient strength. The handle was woven at the apex with leather strips and farther down with grass rope. The grass rope was continued onto the rim as a binding.

The lid is a piece of ¼-inch birch plywood cut to fit inside the handle and notched out to receive the nubs created by the rib ends folded over the rim. It is reinforced on the bottom with a piece of ⅜-inch plywood. The initials were made by cutting through the top ply with a sharp knife and chiselling out this ply to allow the core to show. The platform inside the basket is fashioned with 1-inch-thick legs and a plywood top.

Picnic Basket #2

This is a large basket, measuring 14 by 28 by 11 inches high, but it weighs just 4½ pounds. The double-hinged lid and the double handles are design ideas that have not been dealt with previously. A two-lid system like this is very practical for a large basket, and two handles are ideal for carrying a load that may be unbalanced.

This photo of Picnic Basket #2 shows the laminated handles attached to wooden bosses with wood screws as well as the leather and Velcro closing tabs.

The first step is making a form the size of the basket opening. Around this form I bent the frame pieces for the rim, then the bottom piece of the frame, and lastly the six pieces for the two handles. These pieces were clamped in place around the form and allowed to dry. The frame is put together as shown in the drawing. Note that the two brass "T"s are held in place by the same brass nails that hold the frame together. The eyes and initial weaving were done with ³⁄₁₆-inch binder cane. After I had both sides well started, I commenced weaving in the center of the basket using ½-inch flat cane. I completed the weaving between these two areas with ¼-inch flat cane.

Each of the lids has a solid-wood bar that serves as a foundation for the rattan cane as well as a pivot. See the drawing and photograph for construction details. I started weaving on the lid at both corners with ⅛-inch chair cane and later incorporated some ¼-inch binder cane in the weaving. Before mounting the lids, it is best to complete the handles and attach the space bar. The latter adds strength and keeps the basket's width constant.

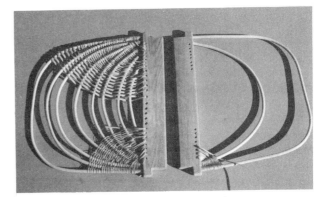

The hinged lids for Picnic Basket #2 are shown here. Four steps in construction are shown. Clockwise from upper right they are: ¼-inch round cane glued into holes in wood bar, fine chair cane woven around these members, the same weaving with additional ribs, and coarser weaving with binder cane.

The handles are glued up from the six white oak strips bent earlier. This is easily done by applying glue and clamping them around the original wood form. Be sure to protect the form with waxed paper or sheet plastic. Sand the laminated

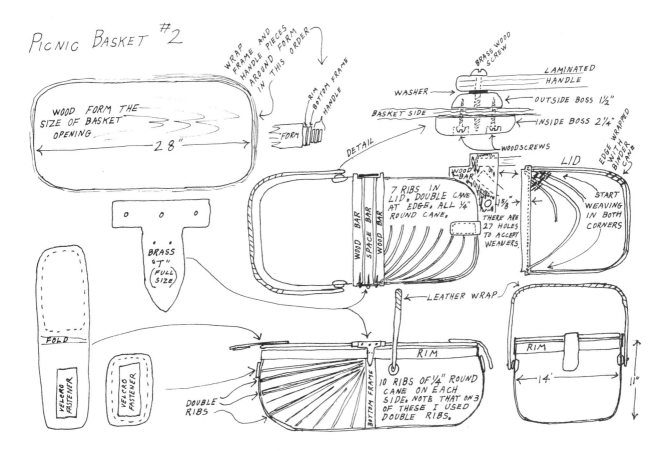

handles smooth and then make eight wood bosses. The four for the inside of the basket are 2¼ inches in diameter and can be made from any tough wood. The bosses for the outside are 1½ inches in size. I made mine from oak to match the other wooden parts of the basket. The bosses are attached to the basket sides from the inside with two wood screws. The handles are then fastened to the bosses with brass wood screws from the outside. Next, attach the lids to the brass "T"s with brass screws. The last job is to stitch the leather fasteners in place on the lids and the ends of the basket. These leather pieces have Velcro fastenings glued to them with contact cement.

Pack Basket

This basket is large but it is simple to make because it is nothing more than a tall version of the Straight-Sided Basket project given earlier in this section. European settlers discovered eastern North American Indians using these packs. They were made of black ash splints which are strong and light. A Pack Basket is comfortable to carry and offers greater protection to its contents than a less rigid pack and thus is ideal for cameras, binoculars, etc. To protect the pack's contents from rain, a waterproof cover can be used or the pack itself can be varnished and the contents placed in waterproof bags. I chose the latter.

The Pack Basket in use. The suede-leather drawstring closure can be seen at the top of the pack.

This Pack Basket was made from 1-inch flat rattan cane. To achieve the stiffness required, I doubled the cane on the corners and on every second or third upright member. The weavers used are ¾-inch cane, with a generous overlap when new pieces were added. This pack measures 9 by 14 by 16 inches high. Weave the rectangular bottom first and then bend the ends up to form the uprights. I skipped two upright members on each pass to make my weaver work. The best shape for this basket is a bit larger at the base so that it will

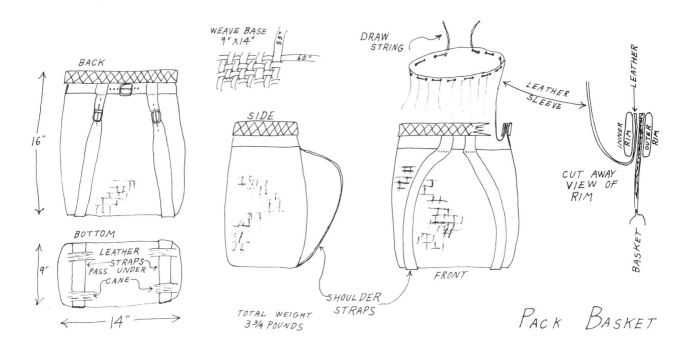

PACK BASKET

The rectangular bottom for a Pack Basket is shown here along with most of the supplies required to complete the project, including an inner and outer rim (*right*), ¾-inch flat cane for weaving (*left*), and leather for shoulder straps (*top*).

fit into the small of your back and a bit smaller near the top to accommodate your shoulders. To do this, gradually tighten up your weaving as you near the top of the basket. When you reach the height you want, point the uprights and weave them back into the basket on alternate sides.

A Pack Basket needs a sturdy rim. I made mine from white oak ⅛ by 1½ inches which was steamed before bending. This basket has both inner and outer rims with the joints on opposite sides. To close the pack, I incorporated a suede-leather drawstring top when I attached the inner rim. The finished assembly consisted of the inner rim, the leather closure, the basket top, and the outer rim. I laced all of these together with leather thongs. By going around twice I achieved the "X" pattern. A thick, sharp awl is the perfect tool to open holes for the lacing.

The author using leather thongs to lace the Pack Basket rim in place.

The two shoulder straps for this pack are 4½ feet long and 2 inches wide. They are made of medium-weight cowhide and have buckles for adjustment of position on the back. They are anchored to a leather belt that is buckled just under the basket rim. The shoulder straps are run under some of the 1-inch cane members on the bottom of the basket to keep them in place.

A Pack Basket is a practical way to carry duffle on the trail, but it also has a certain grace of appearance that makes it unique in outdoor equipment. Finally, it adds a touch of Indian mystique to the popular sport of backpacking.

This is the last of the conventionally woven baskets that will be covered. The following baskets use different techniques or materials that place them in their own special categories.

Island Baskets

I first saw these baskets in New England in 1950. They were so finely made, compared to my rough-textured oak-split baskets, that I determined to learn to make them. I discovered that some setup time was involved but that the weaving was no trick at all. Their history and name apparently go back to the islands of Martha's Vineyard and Nantucket and the light ships near them where these baskets were first made. From the solid-wood base to the oak ribs, these are real wood-workers' baskets. This style can be used to produce items as diverse as small oval baskets and purses to large round picnic baskets. To do this project a form is recommended. For long-term use, make your form of soft wood. To make just a few models, however, a form of glued-up styrofoam or corrugated cardboard will do nicely.

First, decide on the size and shape of the Island Basket you want to make and build a form accordingly. Shape it with saw, rasp, and sandpaper until it is how you want it and the outside is smooth. Then, saw out a base that marries with your form and, with a backsaw, cut a groove ⅜ inch deep all around the edge. The next job, by far the most time-consuming, is the making of the ribs.

My method is to shape the ribs with drawknife, spokeshave, and pocketknife from thick, hand-

The base of an Island Basket with ribs inserted. Around the ribs (*left to right*): a flat piece of oak split for the rim, chair cane, a Styrofoam form, a base plate covered with sandpaper, and a wooden base for another basket.

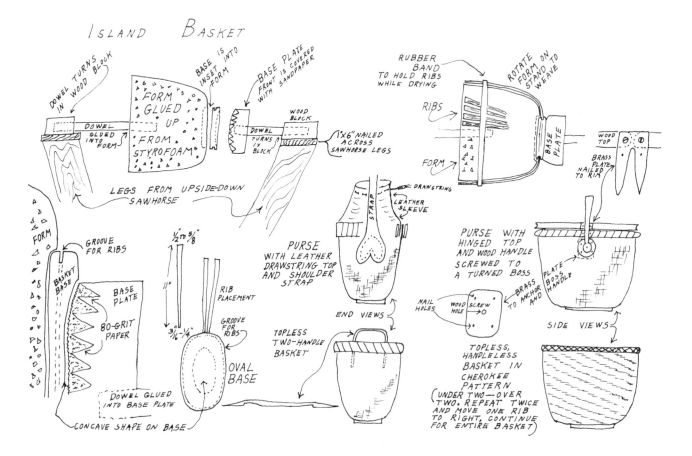

split white oak splits. However, they could be made from ⅛-inch strips cut on the table saw. For each of these Island Baskets, I made 40 ribs 11 inches long. Only 35 to 39 ribs are actually used but it's always well to have replacements for any that break during bending. The finished rib should be about ¹⁄₁₆ inch thick and ½ to ⅝ inch wide at the top and ³⁄₁₆ to ¼ inch wide at the bottom. Test-fit the ribs in the groove in the base. Make sure you have enough to fill the base with about ¼ inch between ribs and that you have an odd number so your weaver will "work." A stand, as shown in the drawing, makes the weaving much easier.

Next, soak the ribs for 24 hours in cold water or two hours in hot water. Insert the ribs in the base and bend them around the form where they are held with strong rubber bands or cord. I mounted the form in my stand during the day of drying so that the ribs were forced into their proper shape. When the ribs are dry they will retain their shape. Remove them one at a time and place just a bit of yellow glue on the small end and reinsert them in the base. When all are glued in place, again tie the ribs to the form and allow the glue to harden.

At this point you are ready to start weaving. Soak a few pieces of chair cane in cold water for 15 minutes and then bend ¼ inch of the cane back on itself and glue this into the groove in the base between two ribs. Start weaving by passing the cane over the ends of the ribs and then pressing it down to the base. Here is my method of adding a new piece of cane. I apply a bit of yel-

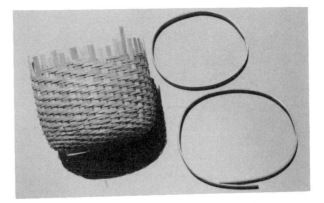

An Island Basket made with what I call a Cherokee pattern. The oak rims for this basket are shown to the right.

low glue to the inside of three ribs and then weave the old and new cane over this. My reason for gluing new weavers in place is that, if the basket is to be used as a purse, the inside will receive as much wear as the outside. The glued ends keep all the weaving tight. Weaving the bottom of these baskets is a little awkward but the trickiest part is where the ribs turn up. If you pull the weaver too tight here it will twist, but if you weave too loose your weaving will be sloppy.

When the weaving reaches 6 to 8 inches in height, you will have to decide what treatment you will use to complete your basket. The choices are a leather top with drawstrings and a shoulder strap, two wooden tops hinged from a brass plate with a laminated wood handle, or a topless basket with or without handles. Regardless of the method you select, you will need a rim. All of these baskets have both an inner and outer rim. These are all of white oak and are flat or half round. The drawings show these four methods. All the rims are fastened with binding and/or brass nails. Rims, handles, and wood lids can be varnished.

Picnic Basket #3

This is a large, round Island Basket with a two-part hinged lid. It utilizes a brass plate with screws serving as hinge pins, much like Picnic Basket #2. Unlike that project, however, this basket has only one handle. I started by turning a base from heavy wood on my lathe and sawing a groove around its edge. The 37 ribs used are 14 inches long and average ¾ inches wide at the top and ½ inch at the bottom. A cardboard form without a stand was used while weaving. The weaver is chair cane.

A chair-cane weaver being passed between the oak ribs on an Island Basket. Observe how the rigid polystyrene form and the base plate hold the basket in place.

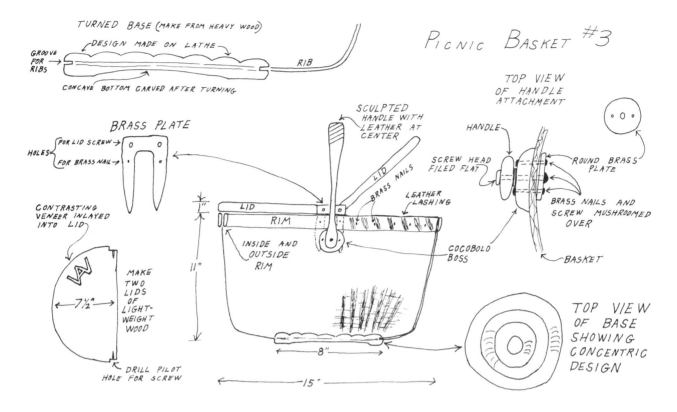

When the weaving reached 10 inches in height, I added both an inside and outside rim. The brass hinge plate is shaped like a double-rooted tooth. It is inserted into the weaving and fastened to the rim and ribs with brass nails. For additional strength, I nailed the rim to every second rib all around the circumference as well as lashing it together with a ½-inch leather strip. The lids are made of lightweight wood and are attached to the hinge plate with brass screws.

The handle on this basket is of laminated holly, one of my favorite woods for bending. The bosses are turned from cocobolo and fastened to the basket with brass nails that pass through holes in a brass disk before being mushroomed over. The handle itself turns on a large brass screw that is also mushroomed over after passing through the disk. One lid was decorated with a logo cut from contrasting wood veneer and inlaid into the solid wood. This entire project was given two coats of brushing lacquer.

Twined Basket

Although a Twined Basket may not look a great deal different from other baskets, it is made by a

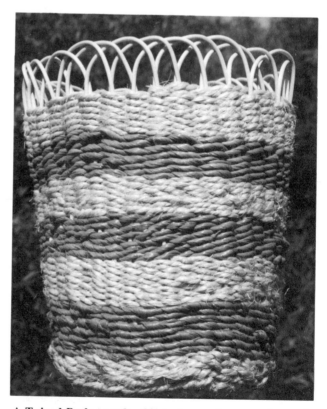

A Twined Basket made of ⅛-inch round cane spokes and sisal and plastic weavers.

unique process and thus deserves a special place in this chapter. This process is defined as "coiling around a support" and that is exactly what you do to construct a Twined Basket. These supports are the standing members of the basket and can be made of rattan cane or splits while the twining material must be very flexible stuff. I used some light sisal rope and some orange plastic cord that was originally used to tie hay bales. Twining uses two weavers which are crossed between each standing member or spoke. If you want a basket with sides that flare out or one with a fancy rim, this is a good design.

The bottom of this basket employs a technique that I have not used on any of the other baskets. It is a bit like the method used to start the Round-Bottom Basket. Twining can be done with an even number of spokes, but I made this basket with an odd number, so you can duplicate it with a single weaver if you desire. To construct the bottom, I crossed two groups of five pieces of ⅛-inch round cane and added one extra piece of cane to make an uneven number. I started twining around the four ends of this cross but soon divided each group of five. This provided nine ends to twine around, counting the odd spoke. I continued twining and eventually broke each group down to individual spokes, so that I was twining

Bottom of a Twined Basket.

around 21 spokes. When the bottom was 7 inches wide I turned the spokes up and proceeded with the twining. When the basket was 1½ inches high I introduced a band of the plastic cord and continued this design until I reached a height of 11½ inches. I incorporated round cane spokes as needed. If I had wanted the side to flare out more, I would have added more spokes and bent them out while twining.

The rim can be completed in a number of ways. My method was simple but added a decorative element to the overall design. What I did was whittle a point on all the spokes. Then each spoke was looped to the third spoke on the left and inserted down into the basket beside that spoke. Proceed around the rim and the basket is finished. I designed this project as a wastebasket, but it could serve in many other capacities.

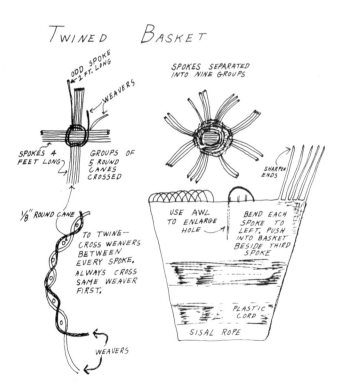

Rim treatment used on the Twined Basket. Each spoke is bent and inserted next to the third spoke to the left.

Coiled Basket

Coiling is a totally different way to make baskets. It is employed all over the globe, with indigenous material used to produce marvelous containers. Watch for them when you travel. Nature will provide you with many materials for making coiled baskets. These include long twigs, pine needles, bark, leaves, corn husks, swamp grass, and the stems of the cereal grains. Purchased supplies, like raffia, jute fiber, grass rope, and waxed string, are another source of materials. Also, consider recycled items like sisal hemp or synthetic rope, cords, yarns, and fibres of all sorts, even rolled-up strips of brown kraft paper.

Long pine needles and linen string are the materials used in this Coiled Basket.

Coiled Baskets. The completed pine-needle basket (*right*) is decorated with red and white beads. Willow twigs and raffia were used to make the basket on the left.

The whole idea of this technique is to feed a continuous coil of medium-strong material into an oval or circle while binding it in place with a very strong thin piece of material. This binder can be quite thin and threaded on a large needle, or a sharpened and flattened twig like willow, or it can utilize a natural point as with a yucca leaf. The binder that holds the coils together can wrap entirely around the previous coil, punch through it, or only catch it at the margin. Also the binder can be wrapped around the coil continuously, so the coil material does not show, or it can be bound sparingly so that the coil material is quite visible. Along with all these variations, different colors and stitching patterns can be used to create designs. A combination used by a number of Southwest Indian tribes are willow twigs or yucca leaves, which are light in color, with the jet black of devil's claw to form animal or geometric motifs.

If the material you select for coils is too stiff to form the very center of the basket, there are various things you can do to remedy the situation. One is to use a more flexible material for the cen-

tral area. Another is to weave a sort of button from the binder material and start the coil around that. You might also consider using a wooden bottom or an elongated shape, which makes it easier to get the coiling process started. Once the coiling is started, you must add material to the coil so that it maintains its normal diameter. For small baskets this will be about ¼ inch, but on larger baskets it might be as thick as ½ inch or even larger. Another variation is to use flattened

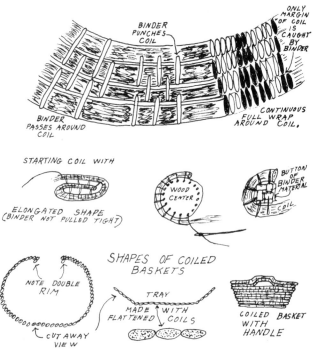

coils that might be ⅝ inch high and ⅜ inch wide. I find working with the basket in my lap to be the most natural position and I have observed that Native American basket makers prefer this position also.

When the bottom reaches the diameter you desire, just start stacking the coils on top of each other to create the sides. The sides can be acutely sloped to form a tray, steeply sloped, or rounded. Rims of Coiled Baskets are often decorated with beads, shells, feathers, or colored fibre. The rim can be made stronger by placing a double coil at or near the top.

Only two examples of Coiled Baskets are shown. One utilizes willow twigs for the coils and raffia for the binder, while the other is made of pine needles with waxed linen string as a binder. I started the bottom of the willow basket with a wood center surrounded by cane and then switched to the twigs with the bark left on. The pine-needle basket is decorated with red and white beads at its rim.

½-inch strips with craft shears. If you have bark from large trees they may measure 4 feet or even longer, but average-length pieces will be around 3 feet. This limits the size of baskets that can be made, but pieces can be joined with contact cement. I use bark strips for projects just as I would use pieces of ½-inch flat cane or oak splits. They can be used as weavers for many of the baskets shown in this chapter. Birch bark can also be used to fabricate an entire basket, as shown by the Straight-Sided Basket in the photo.

The basket with the crenelated rim is of a type we have not covered. I first saw this at a Finnish farm where my wife and I stayed many years ago. This style can be made with other materials, but it is especially well suited for birch bark. Commence the construction by weaving a square base, just as in the first project in this chapter.

The forming of the corners and the turning up of the sides are the distinctive elements about this style of basket. On any normal basket, the corners of this woven base would become the corners of the basket. But, on this one, the middle of the *sides* become the corners. This is so odd, it is

Birch-Bark Basket

This is not a unique style but rather baskets made of a unique material. North American Indians made many clever boxes of birch bark, but I'm not sure if they ever used it to weave baskets. This style of basket making, however, was known in Scandinavia and brought to the New World by immigrants from that area. Birch bark is normally not sold by basketry supply houses so you will have to secure your own. Please read the technical notes in the introductory chapter that deal with this.

Birch bark can be worked green or after soaking in cold water if it has become dry and somewhat brittle. I start by cutting sheets of bark into

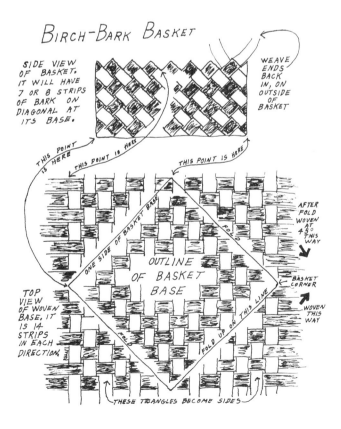

hard for the mind to grasp. To drive the point home, I placed a square piece of wood on top of the woven base in the photo. You may find such a square helpful in forming the corners. The corner of the basket is formed when the strips on either side of the corner of the wooden square are woven together on the diagonal; that is, at an angle of 45 degrees. The triangles of woven base that seem to be left over become part of the sides. The second photo shows this weaving on the bias to form the first corner. Each corner is formed in the same manner. Spring clamps or clothespins may be useful in holding your weaving together while you do each corner. After the corners are formed, continue weaving on the diagonal to complete the sides.

The base of a Birch-Bark Basket with a wood form indicating the four corners. The corner at the top of the photo has been formed and the sides are being woven on the diagonal.

Stop weaving when the shortest strip of bark is 2 inches long. These strips are bent back on themselves and woven into the basket. This exposes the opposite side of the bark which creates an interesting color contrast on the rim. Also, because these pieces approach the rim on the bias, a crenelated or zigzag rim is produced. A Birch-Bark Basket of this type is not only a conversation piece but a practical container that brings a touch of the Great Northwoods into your home.

Slat Basket

This is another unconventional basket. I made this one from handmade oak splits, although ash splints or thin pieces of other flexible woods could have been used. This is an excellent project to use up thin pieces of wood scrap. This example

A completed Slat Basket.

is slightly oval-shaped, measuring 12 by 13 by 4½ inches high. It has a double rim that I made first and held in place with temporary string ties. Next, I bent five slats across the rim about 2 inches apart to form a meager bottom and sides. Then I wove 15 slats around the first five to flesh out the basket.

All these slats were locked in place between the inner and outer rims. I then drilled holes through both rims. These holes were placed so that they included all the ends of the five cross ribs and the ends of every other rib of the 15 remaining ones. Following this strategy, every rivet would pass through both rims with a rib sandwiched between. Next, I set the rivets and removed my temporary string ties. Slat Baskets tend to have rounded bases and thus may not sit straight. See the technical notes for possible solutions. Many variations of slat baskets are possible, including different shapes and the addition of handles. The one shown here is not a fancy example but it was not designed to be anything but a utilitarian fruit basket.

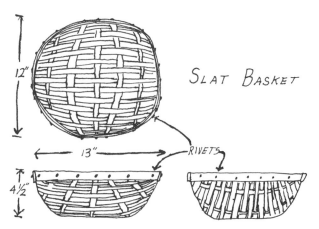

Stick Basket

Here is another unusual basket made entirely of wood. This type of basket can be made square, but I think a better choice would be a hexagon or octagon shape. In any case, it must be a shape with an even number of sides because the sticks are added in alternating sets. To make a hexagon three sticks are attached in each layer, while with an octagon four pieces are needed. I made the base for this project from a piece of white alder. This base has a lower level where the first layer of sticks were attached, but this nicety is not mandatory. For sticks, I used some apricot suckers that I had pruned from a tree the year before. If the wood you select for sticks holds its bark well after seasoning, the bark can be left on; otherwise, it's best removed. If you don't have a source of sticks, use dowels.

This Stick Basket is made in a hexagon shape with sides 4½ inches long. The sticks were cut 6½ inches long and with a 60-degree angle on the ends. If I had selected an octagon the end cuts would have been 45 degrees. These saw-cut ends were trimmed with a pocketknife to give them a rustic chipped look. They were also given a shallow notch about 1 inch from each end. If you want the sides of your basket to be solid sticks, like a log cabin, you will have to cut a half notch. Naturally, if you want your basket to flare out or have some other shape, the sticks will have to be cut to varying lengths. Plan to use the thickest sticks for the bottom layers.

The binder material can be leather, raffia, cord, fishing line, colored yarn, or any other strong material you have. I used rawhide about ¼ inch wide. After soaking and being stretched in place, it was reduced to a width of ⅛ inch. Whatever lashing pattern you employ, stick with it throughout the construction of the entire basket.

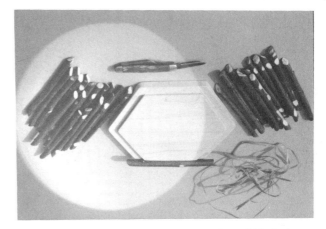

The hexagonal base, apricot sticks, and rawhide lacing needed to make a Stick Basket.

To begin construction, I tied a piece of rawhide to each end of my first layer of three sticks. Then I nailed these to the base on alternate sides. The next layer of three sticks fills in the gaps between the first layer. I lashed the second layer in place and continued adding layers until my basket was 11 sticks high. On larger baskets of this type the sticks can be both lashed and nailed to the layer below. With the top layer tied in place, the project was finished.

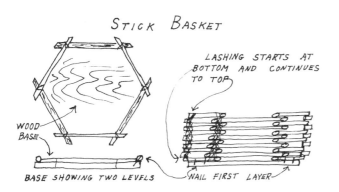

STICK BASKET

LASHING STARTS AT BOTTOM AND CONTINUES TO TOP

WOOD BASE

BASE SHOWING TWO LEVELS

NAIL FIRST LAYER

BOWLS

I am always amazed at the number of top-notch woodworkers who do no turning. It's not that they don't own lathes, it just seems to be a lack of inspiration. Perhaps they turned out a few gavels and then lost interest, so their machines now gather dust. To me they are missing one of the great thrills of working wood. I find the lathe, more than any other power tool, to be the perfect vehicle for a personal creative experience. This may not hold true if you are making exact copies of antique table legs one after the other but it is certainly true when you craft one-of-a-kind bowls.

Let me state at the beginning that I make no claim to being a master turner. But I do enjoy turning and I hope some of this enthusiasm will rub off on you and that you will get some ideas for projects from this chapter. More than the other section in this book, this one concentrates on ideas and downplays techniques. There are many schools of thought on turning. If you are not happy about your turning ability, I suggest you

read what some of the experts have to say about cutting and scraping techniques; do some experimenting on your own, and come up with methods that work for you. That is what I did, and although I know I am not a great turner I have fun doing lathe work, like my results, and that to me is what craftwork is all about. I will describe the steps I went through to produce these projects but I will not try to guide your hand during each turning maneuver.

Historians tell us that the lathe was invented about 3,000 years ago. That makes it a very ancient tool, but its principles are quite straightforward so its early development is not too surprising. Momentum for these first models was provided by hand-activated bows, foot pedals possibly in conjunction with a flexible sapling, or cranks turned by apprentices. I visited Angkor Wat and Angkor Thom in Cambodia in 1960 and noted with interest fancy window bars of soft stone. These intricate bars were obviously made on a lathe and these temples are around 1,000 years old, so I am sure the turner's art is an old one.

A more up-to-date turning story in a rather roundabout way concerns William Shakespeare. His parents' home, which is a few miles outside Stratford-on-Avon, has been preserved. I took a tour of this building some years ago and was fascinated by the stories of how the common people lived in 1564. The barn and shops were of special interest to me because they housed a collection of tools from that era. One item was a lathe of average proportions powered by a hand-cranked flywheel about six feet in diameter. The guide stated that the turner's apprentices had to work that crank for their first five years on the job. I imagine it was a great thrill to be promoted to assistant and escape the backbreaking toil of the apprentice. Perhaps the moral in this for all of us is a greater appreciation of our efficient modern tools.

One of the first Shopsmiths became one of my proudest possessions in the early fifties. These machines included a large-capacity lathe that was well liked for its size but not for the lightness of the machine. My solution was to sandbag the machine, giving it greater stability. I still use this lathe and all of the projects in this book were turned on it. My main reason for bringing this up is to point out that an expensive, fancy machine is not required to do satisfactory lathe work.

This Shopsmith has an outboard turning capability but its normal faceplate turning capacity is so great that I have rarely had to use it. The first bowl that I turned on my lathe was the Checkerboard design included in this chapter. All of my first bowls were turned on either a small or large faceplate but since then I have acquired a combination chuck that I look upon as a great boon to bowl manufacture.

Standards and styles in lathe-made bowls are like the length of ladies' skirts or the width of men's ties in that they are constantly changing. Change is healthy for any art form and I am all for it but I wonder if we don't sometimes paint ourselves into a corner. Not so long ago only flawless blanks were selected for bowl turning and if a hidden flaw presented itself during turning the piece was considered of lesser quality or even discarded. During that period screw holes in the bottom of the project were accepted as a normal part of the landscape. In recent years bowls with every imaginable flaw and even entire sides missing win prizes, but not if any screw holes in the bottom are evident. I see beauty in some of these flaw-encrusted turnings and a few will be found here, but I take exception to downgrading a bowl because it is obvious that it has been near a lathe. My feeling is that such arbitrary standards do not advance the craft of turning one iota.

Another recent trend has been toward thin-walled bowls. There is no doubt that some designs look better with thinner walls, but when turnings become delicate to the extreme I really wonder if we are accomplishing logical goals. It certainly takes skill to turn bowls with cardboard-thin sides, but skill for the sake of skill may not be the best road to follow. Some years ago when all timepieces had mechanical movements, watchmakers kept making them smaller and smaller. Ladies' watches so tiny that they could be mounted on a ring were the result. To make a timepiece so small undoubtedly took great skill, but the watches were not practical because the faces were so minute it was hard to determine the time.

An acquaintance showed me an expensive, thin-walled bowl a few months back. It was superbly made of rare wood but so delicate that he kept it locked up. Although I can appreciate his pride in owning such a fine piece I make my bowls to be useful and to be handled, so you will find little in this chapter about thin-sided bowls. To me one of the great joys of wood is its tactile warmth and to appreciate that a piece must be felt.

So many bowl shapes can be made on the lathe that no book would attempt to cover them all but I have tried to include a wide selection. You may find some of these very much to your liking and others less so. However, an idea book is supposed to present many points of view and that is just what I have tried to do.

Wooden bowls come in all shapes and sizes.

TECHNICAL NOTES

Lathe and Tools

Having done almost all of my turning on one model of lathe I can't offer deep insight on lathe types but I will suggest that you secure the best-quality lathe you can afford, learn as much as you can about it, and maintain it well. If you plan to turn large bowls be sure the machine has an outboard-turning capability. Also check how large a bowl can be turned on its faceplate. If your lathe will be used for between-centers turning, the length of the bed will also be important. The ability of regulating speeds easily and a tool rest that adjusts quickly to all positions are also highly desirable attributes.

Various-size faceplates are available for bowl turning. For many years I used the 3¾-inch and 6-inch sizes that were sold with the original Shopsmiths. Eventually I acquired a combination chuck which I believe to be a wonderful device for any serious bowl turner. My model has jaws that fit into three sizes of depression in the bottom of a bowl as well as a pin-chuck arrangement and a chuck setup that grips the piece to be turned on the outside.

Like most turners I started with a standard set of tools. Mine consisted of three gouges, two skews, a round nose, a diamond point, and a parting tool. This selection worked well and I had hours of turning fun using them. However, as I turned more and larger bowls I felt a need for some specialized tools. Some of these were specific designs for the shaping of the interior of bowls and some were what are usually called long and strong tools. The latter are heavyweight tools that facilitate the hollowing out of deep bowls without the chatter and possible dangers when employing standard tools. My long and strong tool is made of steel that measures ½ by ¾ inch and is 28 inches long. The photo shows a set of standard tools and one faceplate along with some specialized tools and my combination chuck. The two hooked tools are popular in Scandinavia for turning green-wood bowls. Before leaving the topic of tools I must emphasize the importance of keeping them sharp. An occasional grinding on a fine wheel and regular touching up on a fine oilstone are all that are required. These simple tasks will make your turning time more pleasant and result in cleaner work.

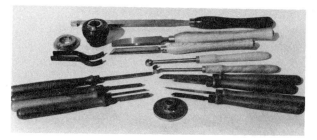

The author's collection of lathe tools along with a faceplate, and combination chuck with its spanner wrenches.

Woods for Turning

Any wood can be mounted on a lathe and turned but some are so superior that they deserve some mention. Most of the well-known cabinetmaking woods including all the varieties of walnut, the hard maples, oak, ash, birch, and the many woods sold as mahogany turn well. Tropical woods especially teak, tulipwood, vermilion, koa, lignum vitae, various acacias, kingwood, zebrawood, padauk, bocote, cocobolo, and ebony are ideal for lathe work. Other American woods that you may want to try are osage orange, elm, hickory, willow, locust, tulip tree, and basswood. I occasionally turn really odd stuff that I find as logs, such as mesquite, desert ironwood, silk oak, carob, Arizona cypress, avocado, and pyracantha. Two woods that add a special dimension to turning are the American and European sycamores and lacewood because of the large pith rays that they display. In Europe sycamores are generally called plane trees. Four fine-grained, light-colored woods that do well on the lathe and deserve greater use are beech, holly, olive, and California bay, which is also referred to as laurel, bay laurel, and pepperwood. In general, hardwoods have a better reputation as turning woods than do conifers but I have turned pine, Douglas fir, various kinds of cypress, and cedars with good to fair results.

If you are an experienced turner I imagine you already have some favorite species. If you are a maverick at the lathe I recommend that you start with stock that is easily available and then experiment with different woods including home-seasoned logs. When I find logs that look as if they have potential for turning I saw the ends straight, coat these ends with oil paint, and stack them out of the weather for a year. If you live in a damper climate you may have to wait two years for logs to season adequately.

Your selection of woods for turning will be affected by many things but color and texture are among the most important. Turning a wood with a marked color contrast between sap and heart tissue is a real thrill because every pass of the tool produces a different pattern. Likewise, when woods with contrasting colors are glued together and then turned, the patterns can be fantastic as well as busy and garish. Color can also be added to turnings by inlaying other woods or by dyeing, painting, or burning.

Yet another source of color is spalted wood. Some species like the maples are especially prone to these bluish discoloration streaks. In my high-school shop class we called this bacterial coloring sap stain and looked upon it as a flaw. Now it is sought-after. Just another case of the changing styles in turning.

Wood textures are more subtle but can still be used effectively to enhance a project. Combining an open-grained wood like oak or mahogany with a tight-grained wood is an often-seen example of this. To heighten the effect the open-grained wood can be used with only the end grain showing. Naturally the normal grain of the wood you are turning will contribute mightily to the appeal of the finished work.

Some woods occasionally show unusual grain patterns. These are seen as a wavy ribbon in walnut and especially in maple, where it shows up as bird's-eyes or a design often referred to as fiddle-back. Burls and wood containing crotch tissue are in a class by themselves when it comes to exhibiting unique patterns.

Along with normal grain and these unusual grain patterns another matter must be considered. This is the orientation of your piece of wood with the tree trunk from which it was cut. I have shown some of these in my drawing. As you can see, the way the bowl blank cuts across the annual rings makes a tremendous difference in the final product.

Mounting a Bowl Blank on the Lathe

I view safety as a paramount feature in turning, and safety starts with the selection of a sound piece of wood and continues with mounting it properly. To mount a blank on the faceplate I square up the end if necessary and band-saw the piece into a circle. If the blank does not lend itself to sawing I attack it with a hand ax. Some may consider this a lot of work to get a round piece, but I would rather sweat a little and have a manageable item than to find later that I was turning a monster. Next I mark and drill small, tapered starter holes for the faceplate screws. Then I attach the blank to the faceplate using round-headed wood screws ¾ to 1 inch in length. On larger turnings I might use even longer screws.

When the faceplate is mounted on the lathe I usually engage the dead center. This not only steadies the work but adds a definite measure of safety. At this point I check the work for round-

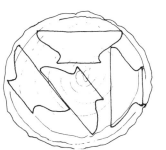

FOUR OF THE MANY POSSIBLE WAYS A BOWL CAN BE ORIENTED WITH THE ANNUAL GROWTH RINGS IN A LOG

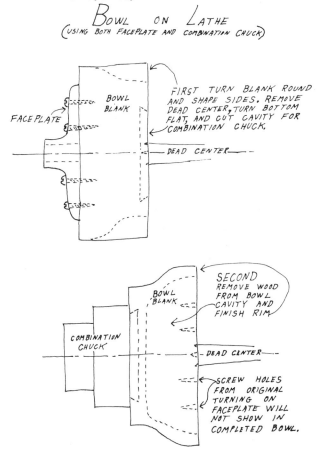

MOUNTING WOOD FOR BOWL ON LATHE (USING BOTH FACEPLATE AND COMBINATION CHUCK)

FACEPLATE

BOWL BLANK

FIRST TURN BLANK ROUND AND SHAPE SIDES. REMOVE DEAD CENTER, TURN BOTTOM FLAT, AND CUT CAVITY FOR COMBINATION CHUCK.

DEAD CENTER

COMBINATION CHUCK

BOWL BLANK

SECOND REMOVE WOOD FROM BOWL CAVITY AND FINISH RIM

DEAD CENTER

SCREW HOLES FROM ORIGINAL TURNING ON FACEPLATE WILL NOT SHOW IN COMPLETED BOWL.

ness. If it is badly out of round I employ draw-knife or spokeshave to correct this problem. Next I adjust the tool rest slightly below the centerline of the work making sure that the widest part of the turning clears the tool rest. This can easily be checked by revolving the workpiece by hand.

Only once have I seen a bowl blank fly apart. The story had a happy ending because the operator was wearing goggles and walked away with just a bump on the forehead. The lessons from the story are plain to see: **don't** mount wood with deep cracks on a lathe and **do** wear face protection. When I start the first rough turning on a bowl I wear a full face mask, a heavy leather apron and sturdy leather gloves. When the piece is nicely rounded I usually discard the gloves but continue to wear the other items.

On many of my turnings I finish the outside and the bottom of the bowl, including the recess that accepts my combination chuck, and then remove the bowl from the faceplate. The next step is to mount the chuck on the lathe and then fasten the work to the chuck. This is accomplished by tightening two rings by hand and then with two spanner wrenches. It's a good idea to retighten this setup after a short period of turning. Other chucks may operate slightly differently but the basic idea is the same. Here again I often use the dead center to steady the work when I start the hollowing-out process. As the bowl cavity becomes deeper I remove the dead center and complete the inside of the bowl.

Turning a Bowl

As I mentioned earlier I don't want to get into theories of turning but a few remarks on procedures would seem to be in order. I start most bowls with my lathe on its lowest speed. Using my largest gouge I work the blank until it is truly round. When this is accomplished I increase the speed and start shaping the bowl still using the large gouge. I like to make my cuts from the widest part of the bowl toward the narrowest. I call this cutting with the grain. Another way to think of it is as cutting downhill, because you cut from high to low. The gouge is a lathe tool used for cutting, which usually results in smoother surfaces. However, the shape of your bowl may re-

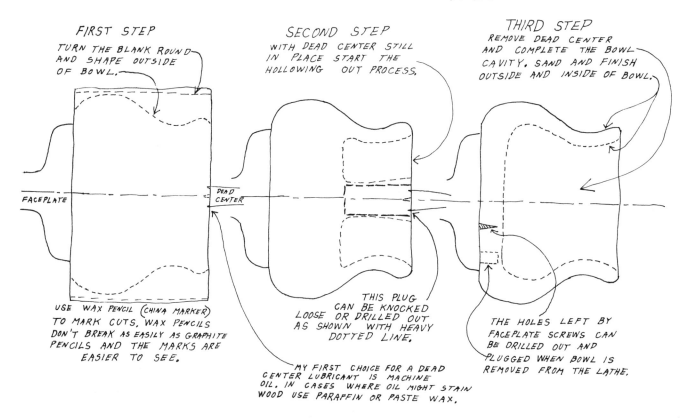

TURNING A BOWL ON THE FACEPLATE

FIRST STEP
TURN THE BLANK ROUND AND SHAPE OUTSIDE OF BOWL.

SECOND STEP
WITH DEAD CENTER STILL IN PLACE START THE HOLLOWING OUT PROCESS.

THIRD STEP
REMOVE DEAD CENTER AND COMPLETE THE BOWL CAVITY. SAND AND FINISH OUTSIDE AND INSIDE OF BOWL.

FACEPLATE

DEAD CENTER

USE WAX PENCIL (CHINA MARKER) TO MARK CUTS. WAX PENCILS DON'T BREAK AS EASILY AS GRAPHITE PENCILS AND THE MARKS ARE EASIER TO SEE.

THIS PLUG CAN BE KNOCKED LOOSE OR DRILLED OUT AS SHOWN WITH HEAVY DOTTED LINE.

MY FIRST CHOICE FOR A DEAD CENTER LUBRICANT IS MACHINE OIL. IN CASES WHERE OIL MIGHT STAIN WOOD USE PARAFFIN OR PASTE WAX.

THE HOLES LEFT BY FACEPLATE SCREWS CAN BE DRILLED OUT AND PLUGGED WHEN BOWL IS REMOVED FROM THE LATHE.

quire the use of the skew or round nose, which are scraping tools. Cuts made by these last tools will probably be less smooth and thus demand more sanding.

Gouges can come into play when hollowing out the inside of a bowl, but more often this job will be done by diamond-point or round-nose tools, or a specialized bowl tool will be used. These particular tools are quite efficient and worth having if you turn many bowls. They are often available in both right and left models. Don't think this is a joke, like the ones about left-handed monkey wrenches. Even though all lathes turn in the same direction, when you hollow out a bowl over the lathe bed you do your cutting on the left edge of the bowl, so you need a left-hand tool. But when you do outboard turning the direction of spin is reversed and a right-hand tool is needed.

If your bowl is large you will probably be able to rig the tool rest inside the cavity. This makes for steadier and safer turning. But if your bowl is quite deep you may reach a point where the tool rest is too far from the cutting face and your regular tools give forth with a lot of chatter. This is where long and strong tools pay off.

The final cuts on both the inside and outside of the bowl should be very light ones. These should be made at a higher speed and with freshly sharpened tools. With practice you can achieve such smooth surfaces that only a minimum of sanding is necessary.

Thus far I have not mentioned the shape of the bowl being turned. In most cases I have a shape in mind and I mark my blank with a wax marker and make my cuts to achieve this design. But once in a while I just start turning and see what happens. Many carvers say they "let the wood talk to them," so the piece being sculpted determines its own fate. Whether you believe this can happen is up to you but I can attest to the fact that this freehand turning is fun. To check inside and outside dimensions and the thickness of bowl walls I use the shopmade calipers shown in the drawing.

Just as there are many ideas about the place of cutting and scraping techniques in lathe work so there are different theories about sanding. I once listened to a lecture on turning during which the speaker stated that abrasive paper must be cut to an exact size and held in an exact way to smooth a turning properly. I got the feeling that he thought if you did it any other way the project

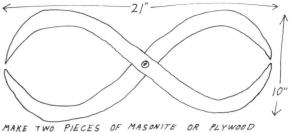

LARGE INSIDE-OUTSIDE CALIPERS

21"

10"

MAKE TWO PIECES OF MASONITE OR PLYWOOD EXACTLY THE SAME, BOLT TOGETHER IN MIDDLE.

would be a disaster and you might get warts to boot. I thought, How silly can experts get?

I sand in many ways with many sizes of abrasive paper depending on the size and shape of the project. Most often I use a single thickness of paper held so the dust is propelled away from me. I should add that I don a dust mask as soon as I start the sanding process. Occasionally I fold the paper once or twice to reach difficult areas. If the paper heats up I may wear a glove or back the paper with a cork pad. A cork pad is also helpful in smoothing straight-sided bowls. I start my sanding with garnet paper using a coarse-enough grit to remove tool marks or other blemishes. For fine sanding I rely on paper coated with silicon carbide or aluminum oxide. Ideally all marks from the last abrasive paper are removed before moving on to a finer one. I usually end up with 600-grit paper but on occasion I go even finer.

Finishing Lathe Work

If you enjoy experimenting with various wood finishes you will have a ball completing the projects you turn. Finishes that demand a great deal of hand rubbing are a piece of cake on the lathe because it does most of the work. Any good book on wood finishing will give directions for some exotic mixtures and unusual procedures you can try. I will describe a few of my favorite finishes but I encourage you to try others. I'll first cover two of the finishes that I favored during my early days of woodworking.

Every craftworker I know who uses rubbed-oil finishes gives them an individual twist, so here is mine. I start by dissolving one part of beeswax in an equal amount of turpentine. Shaving the wax and placing the mixture in the sun will facilitate this. I next mix this solution with six parts of boiled linseed oil and apply this liberally to my project. This is done with the piece on the machine and the lathe bed covered with newspapers. An hour later I apply another lighter coat. After another hour I wipe the turning with a clean cloth, turn on the power, and polish the piece. I use enough speed to warm up the work, which promotes oil penetration. I may also add more oil mix at this time. I continue to polish the project several times a day for the next two days and then remove it from the lathe. I continue by hand-polishing the piece every day for the first week, then once a week for a month.

The other method starts with the application of three coats of good-quality varnish with light sandings between coats. The last coat is sanded lightly with used 600-grit paper and then hand-rubbed with ground pumice in mineral oil using a soft cloth. Don't polish too long or too vigorously as this mix will cut right through the coats of varnish. Next I remove all of the pumice and oil mix and polish the turning with a rottenstone and mineral oil mixture.

In recent years I have often used a variation of one of furniture maker Sam Maloof's finishes on my turnings. To make this I add two tablespoons of carnauba wax chips to one-half cup of tung oil. You will probably have to warm the oil in the sun to get the wax to dissolve. The result is a gooey mixture of honey consistency that I apply with a cloth two or three times and then polish to perfection.

On occasion I finish lathe work with walnut or pecan oil, tung oil, Danish oil, or carnauba furniture wax. I apply these two or three times with a clean cloth about twenty minutes apart and then polish the piece with the lathe running.

Fabricating Bowl Blanks

Many bowls are turned from blanks that are glued together. Probably the most common arrangement is a horizontal stack, that is, a bunch of boards stacked one atop the other. Before stacking, these boards are often cut into circles and perhaps the centers of some of these circles are sawn out. One way to economize on lumber is to use these cut-out centers for narrower lower portions of the bowl. Some turners have worked out ways of cutting these circles with tapered sides, thus achieving an even greater saving of wood.

A less-used method of gluing lumber for bowl turning is the vertical stack. This is simply orienting your lumber in a vertical plane before ap-

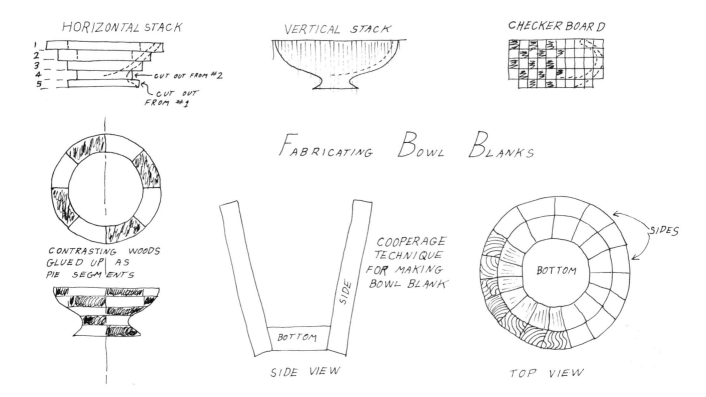

plying adhesives. I utilized this technique for two projects in this chapter. Both of the above methods can be used with similar or contrasting woods.

The checkerboard method of gluing depends on the use of contrasting woods or it would not look like a checkerboard. This has been popular for many years and still yields an interesting end product. The Checkerboard Bowl project in this section uses maple and black walnut but many other wood combinations are possible.

Now let's go back to our original horizontal stack and visualize each wooden circle as a pie. But, to deepen the plot, imagine that we have both apple and lemon pies. We could stack our pies in alternate layers and get a banded effect on the side of the bowl or we could cut the pies in six or eight pieces and intermingle the pieces. As I'm sure you can appreciate, these segmented pieces can be combined in many ways and solid bands can be placed between them to add yet another design.

To really complicate the plot, all of the above gluing systems can be sawn apart at various angles and reglued. The design possibilities are just about endless. Done with restraint the results of such rearrangements can be very pleasing. If done purely for the sake of complex mechanical recombination, however, the resulting bowl can be both tasteless and gaudy.

Still another way to glue up wood for lathe use is by following the techniques employed in making cooperage. This means shaping pieces that correspond to the staves in a barrel and cementing them together. If they converge at the base no bottom is needed, otherwise a bottom must be incorporated when this cooper's stack is glued up. I used this method in the turned Swiss Bucket project.

In doing any of these gluing operations, tight joints are essential. Remember that the pieces you glue together are going to be spinning around on a lathe with your body close at hand. The last thing you want is for all that beautiful wood to go into orbit. So sharpen up your plane and work for tight joints.

Forty years ago when I glued my first bowl blanks I used a variety of adhesives. In recent years I almost always use yellow glue, but on occasion I switch to resorcinol or epoxy. I apply plenty of glue to both surfaces and clamp every-

thing together tightly. After clamping it's a good idea to check that the pieces have really pulled together, and that no clamps have slipped and are applying pressure at the wrong angles. When the glue has set, the blank is mounted and turned like any other piece, except that special care may be required to turn blanks with a lot of end grain showing.

Log Turning

I use this term in a slightly different context so perhaps I should define my meaning. All wood starts as a log so, in effect, every time you use a lathe you are turning a log. But I use this term to mean pieces that are turned with the long axis of the log parallel with the bed of the lathe. I often gather this wood myself and I sometimes leave the bark on the finished project.

The previous paragraph touches on some interesting points. One is that by collecting your own wood you get it free and perhaps even get to enjoy a mountain hike or a walk along the shore at the same time. With the price of turning blanks what it is today any wood that comes to us gratis is a pleasant gift from nature. You also get a chance to season some wood, which is a woodlore experience you may never have been exposed to. Possibly you will want to try your hand at turning green wood and that too may be new ground for you. Lastly, the wide selection of wood that can be gathered as neighbors trim their trees or street crews fell them is wonderful to behold.

I'm sure every woodworker has noticed the unusual pattern on Douglas fir plywood. The wavy grain pattern is the result of the plies being rotary-cut from the logs and that is, in effect, what you do when you turn a log on your lathe. If every log were perfectly round with precisely spaced concentric growth rings, a log turning would be about as dull as a box of mud. Happily, rarely are logs built like that, so you end up with many delightful patterns.

Also log turning is about the only chance a turner has of utilizing the many interesting bark patterns to be found on American trees. I have shown some of these in the project on log turning. I always try to use pieces with tight bark when doing this, but I have found that if the entire cylinder of bark has slipped it can often be glued back in place.

TURNING AHEAD

The projects in this chapter are organized into groups: first, the turning of unglued bowl blanks, then bowls made from glued-up stock, log turning, carved bowls, and unusual bowls. As with the previous topics, I have taken considerable liberty here in my definition of the term "bowl."

If you do much flying you have probably sat next to a "white-knuckle flyer," the type of person who grips the arm rest so tightly their knuckles turn pale. I bring this up because there are also "white-knuckle turners," who have a real fear of the lathe. It's wise to show a healthy respect for power tools but a "white-knuckle" turner must surely lose much of the fun of lathe work, and that is a real shame. Unfortunately, I know of no magic words to reassure these people but perhaps an unbroken stint of turning would help them gain the confidence needed to overcome their fears. I hope the many projects here will provide them with many hours of therapy and eventually pleasure and pride in their work.

Lastly I would like to voice one complaint I have about turning. The modern lathe is such an efficient machine that the time required to finish a project is just too short. I find turning so much fun that it would be nice if, like a good book, it lasted a bit longer. However, like other lathe enthusiasts, I complete one project only to start anticipating the enjoyment I'll have when I mount the next bowl blank on my lathe. It's only a matter of selecting the project.

BOWLS FROM UNGLUED BLANKS

Basic Salad Bowl

This is about as close as you can come to a basic bowl. If you are just getting started in bowl turning it would make an ideal first project. All that is needed is a 6 by 6 by 2-inch blank of fine-grained hardwood like the maple used here. I sawed this into a circle and mounted it on the lathe. This can be done with a faceplate or a combination chuck. The turning was done by first rounding the top and bottom edges with a skew and then cutting the disk into a perfect circle with a medium-size gouge. Next, the hollowing out

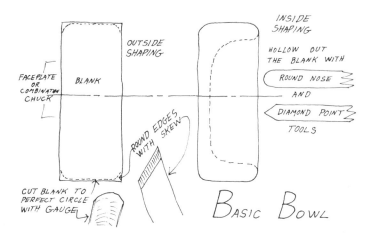

BASIC BOWL

was done with gouge, diamond-point, and round-nose tools. This bowl will hold a medium-size salad. If you like to serve giant salads, start with an 8 by 8 blank.

I finished this salad bowl with walnut oil. After the final sanding I apply a liberal coat and let it soak in for 20 minutes. Then I turn on the lathe and with my bare hands rub in the oil. The heat of the friction promotes this action. I do this at least once more and then, while the bowl is spinning, wipe off any excess oil with a clean cloth. I've found it easy to care for these bowls. After each use I wipe them out with a paper towel, wash them quickly in hot water, and dry immediately. If a bowl appears to be drying out I rub it with walnut oil. Nut oil is, of course, an organic oil and subject to becoming rancid, but I have found over many years that this has never happened to our wooden utensils. This may be because very little oil is actually taken up by the wood, or some neutralizing action takes place in the wood, or simply because we use our wooden items often enough to forestall any problem. Whatever the reason, I believe I can safely suggest using this finish on such hard, tight-grained woods as sugar maple, beech, California laurel, olive, and cherry.

Variations on a Theme

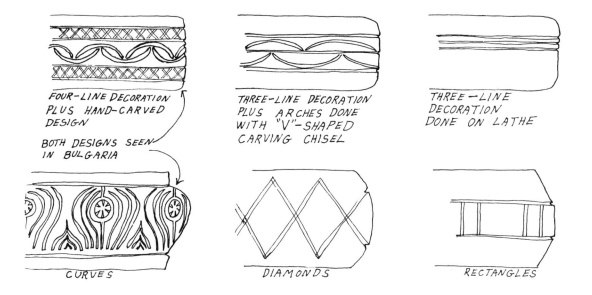

VARIATIONS ON A THEME
METHODS OF DECORATING A BASIC BOWL

FOUR-LINE DECORATION PLUS HAND-CARVED DESIGN

BOTH DESIGNS SEEN IN BULGARIA

THREE-LINE DECORATION PLUS ARCHES DONE WITH "V"-SHAPED CARVING CHISEL

THREE-LINE DECORATION DONE ON LATHE

CURVES

DIAMONDS

RECTANGLES

To add some variety to Basic Salad Bowls, think decoration. The bowl on the left was decorated on the lathe by adding three shallow grooves with a diamond-point tool. This is a time-honored method of applying a design to a turned piece. My preference is for a small number of lines, grouped rather close together, and placed either above or below the centerline. These lines can be darkened by applying pigment or by burning them in with an electric pencil.

The variation on a theme on the right was turned on the lathe where the three lines were added but then it was removed from the machine and hand-carved. The carving of turned projects is quite popular in Europe. In fact this design was inspired by turnings I saw in Bulgaria during the summer of 1991.

Bottle Caddy

Most everyone has had the experience of removing a chilled bottle from the refrigerator, placing it on a polished and beautifully set table, and then had it sweat and drip on everything. A Bottle Caddy prevents this condensation from doing any damage and adds an attractive wooden piece to your table as well. The caddy, of course, can be used for room-temperature bottles and jars also. The uses to which this project can be put are so clever and its manufacture is so simple that I often make a number of them for gifts.

I start with 2-inch stock and band-saw it into a circle about 5½ inches in diameter. An inside diameter of 4 inches will handle most quart or .75 liter bottles, but check the size of your container before doing the turning. The round blank is

A Bottle Caddy and two Mortars and Pestles.

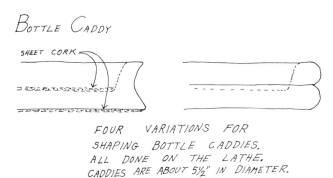

BOTTLE CADDY

SHEET CORK

FOUR VARIATIONS FOR
SHAPING BOTTLE CADDIES.
ALL DONE ON THE LATHE.
CADDIES ARE ABOUT 5½" IN DIAMETER.

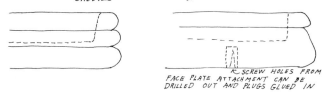

SCREW HOLES FROM
FACE PLATE ATTACHMENT CAN BE
DRILLED OUT AND PLUGS GLUED IN

mounted on the faceplate and turned. A few of
the many shapes and decorations are shown in the
drawing. I usually cut the indentation about one-
half the thickness of the blank. In the case of the
black-walnut caddy shown in the photo, that was
about 1 inch.

No finish that I know of is foolproof around
liquids, especially if they contain alcohol. I have
used polyurethane and rubbed oil on caddies with
satisfactory results. If you have a favorite finish
for use around liquids I suggest you employ it on
your Bottle Caddy. The inside of the caddy can be
covered with a circle of sheet cork to absorb the
condensate. I often put cork or felt on the bottom
of my caddies so they are certain not to mar a
tabletop.

Mortar and Pestle

If you do much cooking you have probably run
into a situation where you needed to crush or
blend spices, herbs, or other ingredients. I used
to try to do this by maneuvering the back of a
spoon in a sturdy dish, with little success. Then I
was inspired to turn some Mortars and Pestles,
and the kitchen has been a happier place ever
since.

The mortars shown in the photo on the previous
page were crafted from olive wood and wild cu-
cumber root and the pestles are both of olive.
Other suitable woods for this project include hard
maple, beech, birch, sycamore, and any of the
hard fruit woods like cherry. These woods impart
little if any flavor to foods and they are hard
enough to crush spices.

The fashioning of a mortar is an easy faceplate
turning project, essentially like the basic bowl.
The pestles are a simple between-centers lathe
project. One thing that is important is that the
inside curve of the mortar and the outside curve
of the bottom of the pestle mate properly, that is,
they must have the same curve to crush spices
efficiently. A cardboard template may come in
handy here. I have shown three designs in the
sketch but many others are possible.

I don't finish the insides of my mortars but I
do feel the outsides need a bit of protection from
the cook's fingers so I usually apply nut oil. In
addition I usually cover the bottom of the mortar
with sheet cork or similar material.

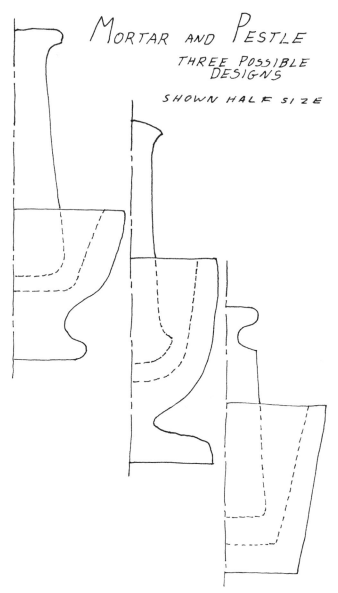

MORTAR AND PESTLE

THREE POSSIBLE
DESIGNS

SHOWN HALF SIZE

Silk Oak Bowl

With the combination chuck attached, the blank is ready to be mounted on the lathe and hollowed out.

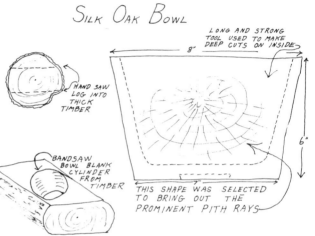

The silk oak (*Grevillea robusta*) is not related to the true oaks in the genus *Quercus* but it does have an attractive wood with large ray cells much like the real oaks. I had a silk oak log and thought about doing a log turning with it, but I decided against it because that method of turning would not show off its beautiful pith rays. I felt the answer was a bowl with a simple design, so that's what I made.

I started by handsawing my log into a timber and band-sawed a cylinder from that. Next I mounted this bowl blank on a faceplate, squared up the bottom, and cut a recess for my combination chuck. With the chucked-up piece on the lathe, I turned the uncluttered shape shown, which displays the annual rings and rays cells very much to my liking.

I envision this Silk Oak Bowl primarily as a container for popcorn or chips but it could be

used to hold a dried arrangement or, with an insert, cut flowers. The bowl in the photo was finished with rubbed oil. If you worry about placing food products in a container that was finished with boiled linseed oil, with its various chemical additives, use nut oil instead.

Sculptured Bowl

The basic shape of this bowl is much like the last project except for the sharper angle of the sides.

Silk-oak blank and the plank from which it was cut, along with a faceplate that will be used to turn the outside.

The similarity ends there, however, as this project has an undulating rim and carved sides. The wood is magnolia, which I don't find terribly exciting in itself, so I used this treatment to give the bowl some life.

To begin, I handsawed a timber from a piece of log and from this I band-sawed a circle with steeply tapered sides. This blank was mounted on a small faceplate and turned into a truncated cone. The piece was not sanded as I don't like to subject my carving tools to grit-impregnated wood. Next I carved the free-form grooves in the outside of the bowl with a ½-inch gouge. The grooves

Sculptured Bowl showing grooves being carved.

were sanded with abrasive paper wrapped around a ½-inch dowel. I did some of the carving with the project mounted on the lathe and some with it removed. If you are carving flutes in a hard wood I recommend that you remove the wood from the lathe to spare your machine the pounding involved in the carving.

Walnut Cuspidor

I didn't necessarily have a cuspidor in mind when I started this project but that's the way it turned out. It's not an unhandsome shape if you can di-

This Cuspidor is complete, except for hollowing out the interior.

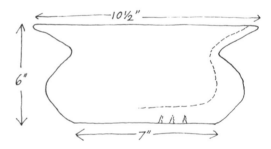

vorce its old function from its modern use, which can be anything from fruit bowl to small wastebasket. I hesitate to call this piece of walnut crotch wood, but a fair amount of it fits that label so perhaps half-crotch wood is the correct term. I was given this large block and cut it down to band-saw size with a handsaw and then cut out a large circle.

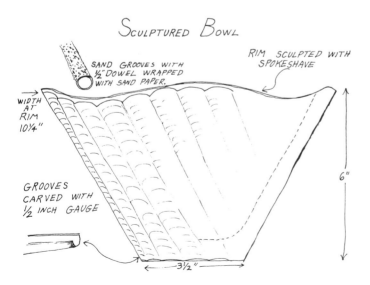

SCULPTURED BOWL

SAND GROOVES WITH ½" DOWEL WRAPPED WITH SAND PAPER.

RIM SCULPTED WITH SPOKESHAVE

WIDTH AT RIM 10¼"

GROOVES CARVED WITH ½ INCH GAUGE

6"

3½"

A large piece of walnut crotch being sawn into slab for Cuspidor.

The blank for the Cuspidor after band-sawing from slab.

The turning was typical of any large bowl except that there was a lot of cross-grained wood resulting from the many branches emanating from this section of trunk. For this reason I ended up using my long and strong tool more than I would have normally. Along with the crotch grain and knots caused by the branches, there were a number of checks but I ignored these because they seemed to belong with this sort of wood. The finish used was my linseed oil and beeswax mix.

BOWLS FROM BURLS

The swirled wood tissue of a burl is marvelous to behold and a treat to work on the lathe. One botanic theory to explain this unusual growth is that something, perhaps a disease, triggers the tree to produce a cluster of bud cells. But the tree has second thoughts and smothers these buds with regular wood tissue that grows in a curly fashion around the buds. Whatever the cause of burls I hope you get an opportunity to turn some of them.

I have had little success in purchasing burls by mail. When they're bought sight unseen, the delivered product can be sad indeed. But I have had loads of fun tramping over my friend's mountain property and sawing them from dead California black oaks. Many other trees produce burls, including maples, sycamores, and redwoods.

Oak burls turned and hollowed out on the lathe.

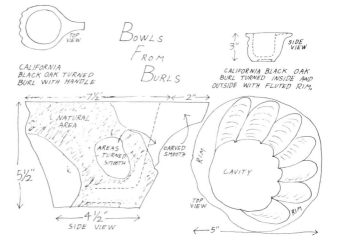

My usual procedure is to mount the side where the burl was cut free on the faceplate. Then I turn the bottom flat, make the indentation for my combination chuck, and shape the outside of the burl. As burls are irregular in shape and may have projections where they were cut free, be extremely careful during the turning process. I sometimes erect a physical barrier in front of my lathe so I can't possibly walk or reach into harm's way in the form of an off-center burl. The grain pattern on a burl is so interesting that I often leave some of it unturned. The shape of the burl will usually dictate what the finished bowl will look like. The photo shows my way of dealing with the large flat surface that can result from an off-center bowl, forming it into a tablike handle.

Relief-Carved Bowl

The ideal bowl for decorating, in my opinion, is of simple design with some flat or nearly flat surfaces for carving. This project does not deal so much with a type of bowl as with a type of decorating. I only discuss here shallow-relief carving, but chip carving as well as inlays of wood, metal, leather, or soft stone are all possible ways of decorating a bowl.

The bowl shown in the photo was turned and carved many years ago from a piece of 2 by 8 black walnut. The design is two intertwined rows of willow leaves. This same basic idea could be used with other leaves, fish, whales, or any other serpentine shape. A vine with leaves, flowers, or fruit encircling a bowl achieves a nice effect. Rows or groupings of flowers will also work well.

Actually the design possibilities are just about endless. Braids, knots, and all manner of fancy ropework are favorite wood-carving motifs and work well on turned pieces. Many themes lend themselves to relief carving, such as horse or cattle heads to portray the American West, anchors and sailboats for a nautical flavor or crossed ice axes and edelweiss flowers for an Alpine touch.

The drawing shows the two common methods of doing relief carving. These two can be combined and on thick-walled bowls you might want to try some deep-relief carving.

Nut-Chopping Bowl

It seems that everyone in our family likes to cook and bake. Much of this cooking is done from scratch, which means we chop lots of nuts. Over the years we tried several devices for doing this but they all either broke or proved unsatisfactory. At last, in desperation, I turned a Douglas-fir bowl with an inside shape that exactly matched a cross-handed chopping knife I had made. This setup chopped nuts and other foods so effectively that we are still using it many years later. The rather odd-shaped knife is called an Eskimo woman's knife, or ulu. It is an extremely efficient tool that can also be used to work leather. This one was made from a piece of saw blade that was shaped with a cutting torch, ground to shape, and then tempered. A similar instrument, sometimes with more than one blade, can be purchased in kitchen supply shops.

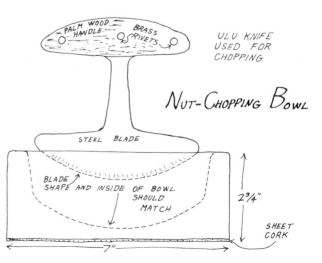

This is a simple faceplate lathe project. The one important consideration is to shape the inside of the bowl just like the chopping blade to be employed. To do this I made a cardboard template of my knife blade and used it as a guide while shaping the inside of the bowl. As would seem fitting, this project is finished inside and out with nut oil.

Four American woods are ideal for this Nut-Chopping Bowl. They are rather hard woods and tend to be taste neutral, so they can come into contact with foods and not impart a foreign taste. The woods are hard maple, sycamore, beech, and birch. As I did not have a suitable piece of any of these when I turned this bowl, I used Douglas fir, which has served well.

Wooden Plate

A few hundred years ago the Wooden Plate was a common item in many homes and was actually used at table. Now they are valuable antiques in this country but still made in Europe and sold as souvenirs. I fashioned this project somewhat in the European style and painted it with bright colors as they usually do.

The turning of a plate is just like turning a shallow bowl. Mount your blank, which only needs to be about an inch thick, on the faceplate with short screws. Turn the sloping sides first and then the inside. A few ridges or incised lines can be included on the face of the plate. These act to divide the plate into areas for decorating. This can take the form of painting, burning with an electric pencil, carving, or some combination of the three.

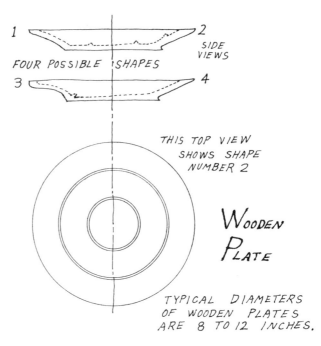

The Wooden Plate shown here is of maple. It was painted with acrylic enamel and then given a coat of varnish. It was designed to be a wall decoration, but can be used to serve crackers, snacks, or fruit, or as a dresser-top accessory.

Branded Bowl

Branding, that is, burning, is an easy and distinctive way to decorate a bowl. You can use a commercial electric pencil, a soldering iron, a steel wire mounted in a wooden handle, or other long piece of steel. Work carefully and wear gloves as it's easy to get burned. The motifs can be from nature, sports, history, or geometric patterns and

Branded Bowl

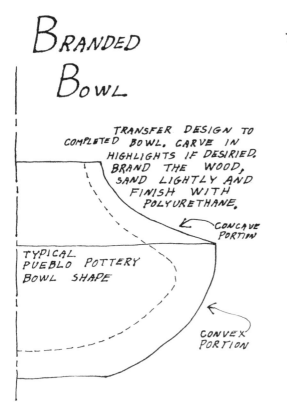

TRANSFER DESIGN TO COMPLETED BOWL. CARVE IN HIGHLIGHTS IF DESIRED. BRAND THE WOOD, SAND LIGHTLY AND FINISH WITH POLYURETHANE.

CONCAVE PORTION

TYPICAL PUEBLO POTTERY BOWL SHAPE

CONVEX PORTION

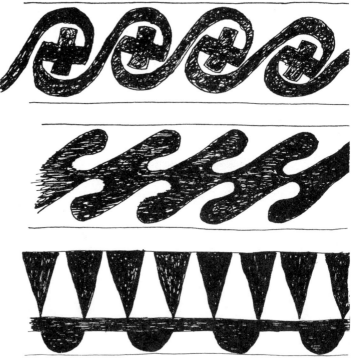

THREE POSSIBLE DESIGNS

can feature a few bold shapes or a plethora of designs. Before branding, the designs can be incised with a rotary burr or regular carving tools.

This bowl was turned from a maple blank measuring 8¼ by 4½ inches. It is a basic faceplate operation with a few new twists. The shape utilizes what I call the concave–convex formula. In this formula either the top or the bottom portion of a bowl is concave and the other portion is convex. I like to divide these two shapes not in the middle but rather with a ratio of about 60 to 40. In this case I placed the 60 percent convex portion on the bottom. I used a dead center until I had shaped the outside. After removing the dead center I hollowed out the bowl with tools including diamond-point, round-nosed, long and strong and a special bowl design. The opening at the top is 2 inches wide, which might seem a bit small but which is quite large enough to allow you to make the bowl cavity. Proceed with care, make light cuts, and don't lose your concentration.

Quite a few years ago I visited the San Ildefonso Pueblo and met the famous potter Maria Martinez. Struck by the beauty of her creations, I tried with this bowl to reproduce a piece of Pueblo pottery in wood.

BOWLS FROM GLUED-UP STOCK

Bud Vase

A bud vase is ideal for displaying a few small flowers and it is a very easy lathe project. One, two, or three buds always seem to look great in these low containers. For the vase to hold fresh flowers you will, of course, have to drill a hole to hold a glass or plastic tube. Dried material requiring no water tubes also looks fine in a bud vase. Another idea is to drill several holes in the top of the vase so it can be used for a nosegay type of arrangement.

This Bud Vase was made from two pieces of maple burl that were glued together. The pieces measured roughly 6 by 6 by 3 inches. The glued-up blank was mounted on the faceplate and shaped into a spheroid. I sanded the piece and finished it with walnut oil. After removal from the lathe I drilled a ¾-inch hole deep enough to hold a watertight plastic tube.

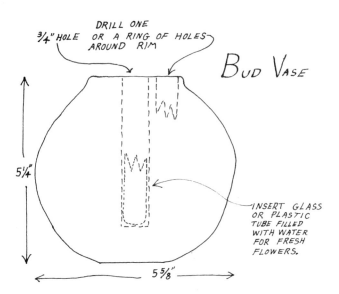

Glued with resorcinol, this Teak Salad Bowl has been in use over thirty years. The utensils are made of mahogany.

This is the first project in this chapter to utilize glued-up stock. It is a two-piece horizontal stack and is probably the simplest example of a glued bowl blank. In subsequent projects we will explore much more complex methods of gluing up stock for turning projects.

Teak Salad Bowl

I turned this bowl a number of years ago. It's a rather straightforward lathe project but there is an interesting story on how I acquired the wood. One of my fellow professors owed me a favor so he

asked me one day if I would like a grand piano crate he had in his barn. Crates are normally made from the poorest grade of lumber but I didn't want to hurt my friend's feelings so I said okay. That turned out to be the right thing to say because the crate was made of teak. It seems that my friend's brother had been working in Burma and when he was transferred home the local mover packed his piano using the cheapest local wood. I'm glad he did because I used the wood from that crate to make a Danish modern chair, two salad bowls, and a cutting board.

I had heard that teak, because of its wax content, was difficult to glue. Back in the fifties, glues were less sophisticated than today and I was a bit apprehensive about gluing teak for a salad bowl that would be subject to repeated washings. I decided to try resorcinol. The bowl is now thirty-five years old and has been washed hundreds of times with no problems whatsoever.

To construct the bowl I first glued up crate pieces to form boards and cut circles from these. Incidentally, the triangular scrap pieces from these

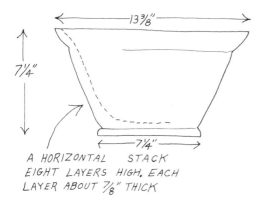

Teak Salad Bowl

13⅜"

7¼"

7¼"

A HORIZONTAL STACK
EIGHT LAYERS HIGH, EACH
LAYER ABOUT ⅞" THICK

circles were glued into a horizontal stack and carved into a sculpture which can be seen on the step above this bowl in the group photo on page 112. A coping saw was used to cut the interiors out of the larger circles and these were used for the base of the bowl. Once the blank was glued into a typical horizontal stack it was mounted on a faceplate and turned. I can't remember what finish I used but it was probably walnut or pecan oil.

Key Tray

Where do you put the stuff you take out of your pockets at night? This tray is one answer. It's wide enough and deep enough to hold keys, change, wallet, pocketknife, watch, date book, and beeper. A lady might find such a tray useful when changing purses, sorting jewelry, or to hold business cards.

This Key Tray is an easy turning project that can be crafted from almost any wood. I had a wide piece of ash that I thought would be ideal for this project but it was already glued to a piece of pine. Instead of presenting a problem, I sawed a disk from this piece of wood and used it for the tray.

I mounted the biwood disk on a faceplate and completed the turning in short order. Note that the tiny tray side has a distinct lip which makes it easy to hold even with one hand. The tray was given a rubbed-oil finish with my mixture of linseed oil and beeswax.

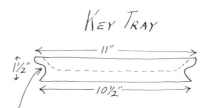

Key Tray

11"

1½"

10½"

DEEP RECESS TO
PROVIDE GOOD GRIP

Inlaid Bowl

This project had an inauspicious beginning. I had a piece of 1-inch Honduras mahogany on hand and another piece of 2-inch stock. Since both pieces contained some flaws, I decided to cut them into circles and glue them up to make a bowl blank.

I turned the bowl and the wood was attractive but the bowl seemed to need something. After casting about for inspiration, I thought I might try circular inlays. My first choice for inlay material is oak root because of its showy pith rays, but I didn't have any seasoned pieces. What I decided to use were creamy pieces of beech cut with a

Concentric mahogany rings that will be used to fabricate the Inlaid Bowl. The outside was cut with a band saw and the inside with sabre or coping saw.

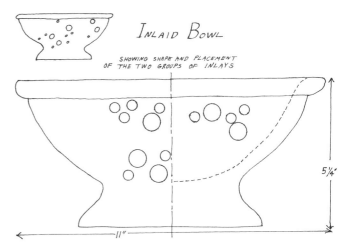

INLAID BOWL

SHOWING SHAPE AND PLACEMENT OF THE TWO GROUPS OF INLAYS

5¼"

11"

A bowl blank, glued as a horizontal stack and mounted on the faceplate ready for turning.

A scrap piece was temporarily glued in the open end of this bowl blank to accommodate the dead center.

⅝- and ⅜-inch plug cutter. The beech provided a strong color contrast with the darker mahogany which was just what I wanted. A more pronounced textural contrast could have been achieved by using birch dowels with the end grain showing.

Inlays on two sides seemed like a good idea, but I wanted them to be completely natural, that is, laid out in a random fashion. To do this I splashed some water on the turned bowl. Where a large drop hit the project I drilled a ⅝-inch hole and where smaller drops hit a ⅜-inch one.

These inlays were affixed with epoxy, then rasped down a bit and sanded flush with the lathe running. The Inlaid Bowl was finished with my linseed and wax mixture.

Vertical Stack Bowl

This salad bowl, with its 14½-inch diameter, represents the largest size that can be turned over the bed of my lathe. I would say the vertical stack is

Vertical Stack Bowl

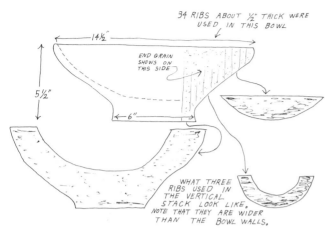

34 RIBS ABOUT ½" THICK WERE USED IN THIS BOWL

14½"

END GRAIN SHOWS ON THIS SIDE

5½"

6"

WHAT THREE RIBS USED IN THE VERTICAL STACK LOOK LIKE. NOTE THAT THEY ARE WIDER THAN THE BOWL WALLS.

The drawing shows three of the rib shapes used to glue up the vertical stack. The remainder of the ribs are intermediate between these three examples. I make all the ribs extra-wide so I'll be sure to have plenty of material to work with. The adhesive was yellow glue. Although Philippine mahogany is a soft wood it can be fibrous, which causes a fuzzy surface when turning, so I kept my tools extra-sharp throughout this operation.

The outside was turned first and then the inside which was largely hollow because of the rib construction used in the vertical stack. The Vertical Stack Bowl was sanded smooth and finished with salad-bowl lacquer.

less popular than the horizontal stack for constructing bowl blanks but it is a viable method and it should be in every turner's repertoire. The wood used was light and dark Philippine mahogany slightly under ½ inch thick.

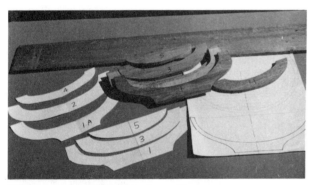

Plans, templates and ribs that will be glued up for a Vertical Stack Bowl.

Overhead view of a Vertical Stack Bowl blank.

Outboard-Turned Bowl

Any chapter on lathe work, in my opinion, must contain an outboard turning project. This project is a big salad bowl made from scraps of fir subflooring 1 inch thick.

To do outboard turning on most lathes you need only to mount the work on the side of the machine away from the bed. However, on my Shopsmith I had to remove the motor unit and reverse it on the bed. This is a heavy job but not all that difficult. Outboard turning also means setting up a freestanding tool rest. This bowl was turned with standard tools but if you plan to do a great deal of outboard turning you might consider the acquisition of a right-hand model of a special bowl tool, unless you have a Shopsmith which uses a left-hand tool.

I worked up templates for the pieces of fir needed for the vertical stack, sawed them out, and glued them together into a large bowl blank. The

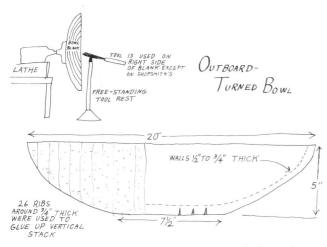

OUTBOARD-
TURNED BOWL

LATHE
BOWL BLANK
TOOL IS USED ON RIGHT SIDE OF BLANK EXCEPT ON SHOPSMITH'S
FREE-STANDING TOOL REST

20"
WALLS ½" TO ¾" THICK
5"
7½"
26 RIBS AROUND ¾" THICK WERE USED TO GLUE UP VERTICAL STACK

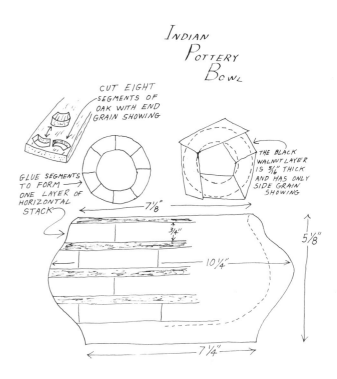

INDIAN POTTERY BOWL

CUT EIGHT SEGMENTS OF OAK WITH END GRAIN SHOWING

GLUE SEGMENTS TO FORM ONE LAYER OF HORIZONTAL STACK

THE BLACK WALNUT LAYER IS 5/16" THICK AND HAS ONLY SIDE GRAIN SHOWING

7⅛"
¾"
10¼"
5⅝"
7¼"

circumference was band-sawed into a circle and the bottom was flattened so that it could be screwed to a large faceplate. After mounting I took special precautions to make sure that all was safe and in readiness for turning because I knew the rim of the bowl would be really flying when I turned on the power. Even at my slowest lathe speed the roar of this blank was quite impressive.

The freestanding tool rest, the large size, and the extreme speed of the perimeter of the bowl make outboard turning a unique experience. But the actual turning was not a great deal different from making a large bowl over the lathe bed. A few extra precautions, like checking the tightness of the screws on the faceplate and testing the soundness of the glue joints, are in order. After sanding, the bowl was finished with nut oil.

Indian Pottery Bowl

Having been a student of Native American lore since I was a kid, I fell in love with the many tribes and villages I visited after moving to the Southwest. I was especially attracted to their many colorful crafts, including pottery, and even tried my hand at duplicating it on the potter's wheel. Unfortunately, my enthusiasm always surpassed my ability and the clay would end up splattered on the wall. I have, however, tried to get some of the shape and feeling of their pottery into this project.

This bowl is constructed of segmented pieces of oak cut so only the end grain shows and thin pieces of black walnut placed so only the side grain is evident. This is a fine project to use up scraps of any two contrasting woods you have around the shop. The combination of oak and black walnut is especially suitable because the end grain of oak has a coarse, open texture as opposed to the tight grain of the walnut. The color contrast between the two woods is obvious but I also wanted a difference in the thickness of the two woods, a touch reminiscent of the thick and thin stone layers often used on Indian buildings. With yellow glue I glued up the pieces, one layer at a time, in a horizontal stack, being careful to alternate the joints just as in laying bricks.

End-grain oak is tough stuff, so sharpen up your lathe tools before starting this bowl. I finished this project with my tung oil and carnauba wax mix. It could hold a dried arrangement in the living room, chips or popcorn on the patio, or pot holders in the kitchen.

Pedestaled Candy Dish

This bowl of mixed mahogany and oak was designed to hold after-dinner mints but it could function as an all-around candy dish, a small fruit bowl, or for serving other snacks.

The blank was glued up in the normal horizontal stack using oak pieces just a bit over ¼ inch thick and mahogany stock around ¾ inch. The first step was gluing the oak to the mahogany and then fastening all the disks together. The bottom two pieces of the pedestal were sawed from inside the top disks. They do not have an oak layer between them. Yellow glue was used throughout this project.

The turning was done in my standard method by mounting the base of the bowl on a faceplate and engaging the dead center in the top of the bowl. I had to glue a wood circle in the center of the bowl opening, however, so that the dead center could make contact. A rubbed-oil finish was used.

Checkerboard Bowl

This bowl was turned in the late forties. Gluing up contrasting woods to form a pattern for a turned bowl was not unknown at that time but it was not nearly as popular as it is today. Also the technology was quite unsophisticated. The ¾-inch-square pieces of black walnut and hard maple were bonded with Weldwood glue.

The design of the bowl was kept simple so the checkerboard pattern could carry the project. I first cut my stock to size and glued up the two solid bottom layers. The following two layers were glued up with a hollow center as per the drawing. After gluing, the blank was sawed into a circle on the band saw and turned on the faceplate into this basic but functional shape. Skew and diamond-point tools were used to cut the inside circumference on the rim of the bowl. The piece was finished with three coats of varnish, then rubbed with pumice and rottenstone.

I have used this Checkerboard Bowl for years

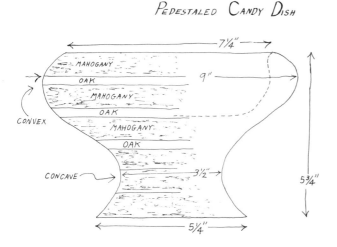

PEDESTALED CANDY DISH

7¼"
MAHOGANY
OAK
9"
MAHOGANY
OAK
MAHOGANY
OAK
CONVEX
CONCAVE
3½"
5¾"
5¼"

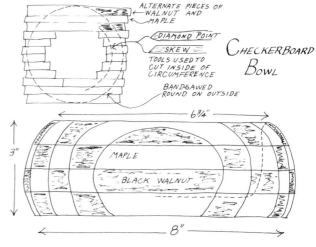

ALTERNATE PIECES OF WALNUT AND MAPLE

DIAMOND POINT
SKEW
TOOLS USED TO CUT INSIDE OF CIRCUMFERENCE

BANDSAWED ROUND ON OUTSIDE

CHECKERBOARD BOWL

3"
6¾"
MAPLE
BLACK WALNUT
8"

to hold change and keys on my bureau. The rubbed-varnish finish has held up beautifully. One remark about this bowl will point up the rarity of turnings of this type in the forties. Shortly after finishing this project it was sitting on a table in my parents' home. A friend who knew I had a lathe saw it and remarked that he thought I had done a neat job of painting the squares on the bowl.

Square Tray

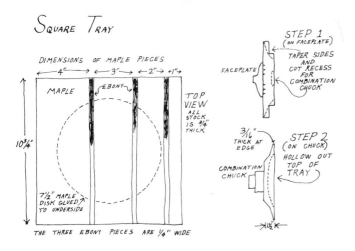

Many variations of this striking design are possible by employing different woods in different patterns. This design utilizes a vertical stack of maple and Macassar ebony for the top laminated to a solid maple bottom in a horizontal stack. Such a tray might be used to serve mints or snacks, as a desk accessory, or as a container for keys and change.

I started by gluing the maple and ebony pieces together and then attaching the round maple bottom. Before turning I trimmed the top piece

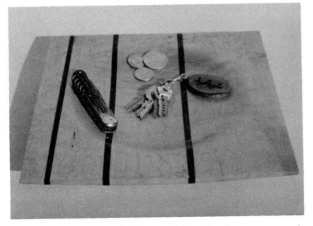

square on the table saw. A large faceplate was affixed with short screws to the top of the tray. This allowed me to taper the rounded bottom of the tray as well as the square top section. At this time I also cut a recess for my combination chuck in the bottom of the tray. As in all cases where a square piece is mounted on a faceplate, be especially careful of those four spinning corners.

I then removed the faceplate and mounted the tray on the lathe with my combination chuck. This allowed me to hollow out the tray. The object here is to remove enough wood so the faceplate screw holes don't show and to provide sufficient recess so the project will perform as a functional tray. After sanding, the Square Tray was finished with polyurethane.

Tanzanian Basket-Design Bowl

As the title indicates, this bowl was inspired by the sisal baskets we saw in Kenya and Tanzania a few years back. The nicely made baskets featured exuberant designs and often used the stair-step splashes of a contrasting color that I have tried to duplicate.

I started by ripping a maple 1 by 6 down the middle at a 45-degree angle and then cut a padauk 1 by 3 on both edges with the same saw setting. Next I glued the padauk piece between the two maple pieces. In doing this I clamped strong, straight braces wrapped in plastic on either side of the glued-up stock, to be sure the 45-degree angles did not slip during clamping. The glued-up boards were planed flat and band-sawed into six circles. The inside portion of the two largest circles became the smallest circles used on the top and bottom of the bowl. The circles can

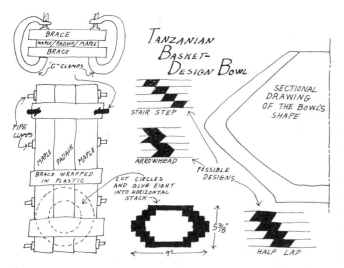

be glued together to make a number of interesting patterns such as the stair-step, which I employed, or a half lap, or an arrowhead design. You will note that the opposite side of the bowl will have your design more or less in reverse.

Although affixed to a faceplate, the turning of this project involves some elements that we haven't as yet covered. The bowl blank is hollow but has solid ends so I was able to use the dead center for stability during the turning of the outside. I did almost all of this outside turning with my largest gouge, which I had just sharpened. It was fun to see the design come to life as the turning progressed. When the outside was completely shaped and partly sanded, I cut a 2¼-inch hole in the end with a small skew. This plug will push harmlessly into the cavity of the bowl and presents no danger. It can be easily removed when the lathe is stopped. Of course, this procedure signals the end of the usefulness of the dead center, which can be removed.

Some of the maple and padauk used to make the blank for the Tanzanian Bowl.

I used round-nosed, long-and-strong, and special bowl tools to turn the inside of the bowl. The 2¼-inch opening may look small but it is plenty big enough to allow you to complete this job. If you don't have a long-and-strong lathe tool, positioning the tool rest with one end in the bowl opening may prove helpful. However you set up your tool rest, make light cuts and proceed carefully and you should be okay.

The sanding of this bowl was completed with 600-grit paper. It was then given three coats of polyurethane with light sandings between coats and finally rubbed with pumice and then rottenstone. I used polyurethane on this bowl to keep the vibrant red of the padauk from weathering to its normal burgundy.

BOWLS TURNED DIRECTLY FROM LOGS

Weed Pots

This is one of the simplest forms of log turning so I'll cover it first. I even leave the bark on some pots so that there is no doubt they came directly from a log. Of course, Weed Pots can be turned from pieces cut from timbers or from glued-up blanks. They are fast and fun to make and they are greatly appreciated as gifts.

I'm not sure if there is an accepted definition of "weed pot." To me, it is a small turning with a narrow opening designed to hold dried weeds or other such material. I turn several styles most of which are shown in the photo and drawing. The ship's decanter or captain's flask has nice flaring lines with its heavy bottom and delicate neck.

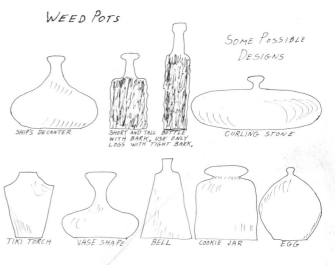

A number of weed pots all turned directly from logs.

The bottle shapes that display a lot of bark gain their appeal from their very rusticity. All of the weed pots, although plain in design, have a definite charm about them. If none of the designs shown here strike your fancy, you're more than welcome to come up with some shapes of your own.

I turn Weed Pots both between centers and between faceplate and dead center. As far as woods, I use just about anything I can lay my hands on. The woods employed in the pots in the photo are, from left to right, camphor, alder, avocado, pyracantha, Asian persimmon, and pine burl. After completion of the turning I bore a hole from ½ to ¾ inch in diameter in the top. I use a wide range of finishes on my pots including stains, paste wax, Danish oil, or nothing at all.

Mesquite Vase

There is a strong sense of anticipation when a piece of two-tone wood like mesquite is mounted on the lathe. What form will the patterns between the creamy-white sapwood and the chocolate-brown heartwood take? You won't know until the piece is turned so the project results in double

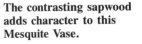
The contrasting sapwood adds character to this Mesquite Vase.

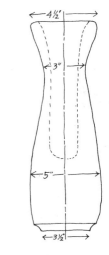

fun. First you get the enjoyment of the turning and secondly the expectation of a beautiful pattern. Many tropical woods as well as black locust, redwood, walnut, and some of the cedars have a marked contrast between heart and sapwood and lend themselves to this sort of turning.

I turned this piece between centers and hollowed out the open end as well as possible while the project was on the lathe. After removing the vase from the lathe I drilled and chiseled some additional wood from the opening.

This particular piece of mesquite was picked up in the desert several years ago and like most such pieces had a number of worm holes. These can be viewed as flaws, making them a liability, but I prefer to think of them as assets in that they add texture to a project. Unfortunately, I had to remove more of the creamy sapwood than I had intended to achieve a pleasing shape. The Mesquite Vase is finished with Danish oil.

Bone-Inlaid Goblet

The goblet is an interesting shape for a turning project. This is an oversized example with rather plain lines, but they can be made smaller and with more intricate designs. Wood goblets are often made simply for display, however they can also hold candy sticks, or pencils on a desk. A glass or plastic insert can also be used if you want one of your creations to hold fresh flowers.

This project was turned from a slow-grown log of western cedar. The base was mounted on a small faceplate and the dead center was engaged for the initial turning. The shape of this goblet brings into play the concave-convex formula that I

mentioned previously. After the bone inlay was completed the dead center was removed and the goblet was hollowed out.

The idea of using bone to inlay a turned piece, a jewelry box or any other crafted wood item may never have occurred to you but bone is a marvelous material. It can be sawed, drilled, sanded, and polished just like any hard, dense wood. I have never worked ivory but I have been told that bone has many similar working characteristics. That's a lot to say for a material that comes to us gratis via the butcher shop and kitchen. If you are a vegetarian I hope you have some meat-eating friends who can supply you with inlay material. Large beef bones are my favorite, but don't neglect those from sheep, elk, bison, etc. The bones can be used whether raw or cooked. Simply clean them up and they are ready to be crafted.

The thunderbird is a Southwest Indian design and one that I admire. I first fashioned this 2½-inch-high thunderbird from a piece of beef bone and then scribed its outline on the side of the turned and sanded goblet. Next, the cedar was carved out with small chisels so the bone figure could be epoxied into the cavity. When the epoxy had set up, the bone was first rasped down almost to the level of the wood and then the lathe was turned on and the bone sanded flush with the wooden goblet. The goblet was then darkened with black leather dye to bring out the ivory-colored bone inlay. Wood dyes have not been discussed thus far in this book but they offer many interesting finishing possibilities and I encourage you to experiment with them. In this case the dye allowed the intricate cedar grain pattern to show through ever so slightly, which I think gives it a nice effect.

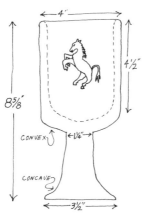

An inlaid bone thunderbird sets off this dyed-cedar goblet, but you can use any motif you choose.

TURNING GREEN WOOD

All of the projects thus far in this section have been turned from seasoned wood. Turning unseasoned wood is easy in that many woods cut faster when they are green and if some precautions are taken in drying the bowl, the results can be satisfactory. An avocado log only a few days away from being a tree was used for the following project.

Fluted-Rim Bowl

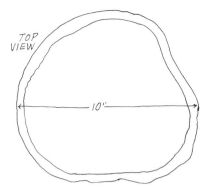

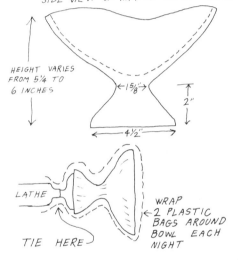

The log was first tapered with an ax and then it was fastened to a faceplate and the dead center engaged. Seasoned avocado is a soft and easily turned wood but when green it cuts with even less effort. My plan for this log was to turn a pedestaled container for serving snacks. I roughed out the outside one day and wrapped the bowl in two layers of plastic. The next day I hollowed out part of the cavity but still left the sides about 1 inch thick. My slowness in completing the turning was calculated to allow the wood to season somewhat as I went along. Again I protected the wood with plastic during the night. The following day I worked the sides and bottom down to around ⅜ inch thick. I neglected, however, to cover the

An avocado log that has been tapered with an ax prior to mounting on the faceplate.

turning that evening and considerable warping occurred during the night. I rather liked the fluted-rim edge so I sanded and waxed the bowl and proclaimed it finished. Other green woods given the same treatment might have developed a few large cracks or many small checks.

My finished turning was still not really seasoned so I placed it in a plastic bag and left it in a cool room. Over a period of two weeks I first opened the bag slightly, then fully, and finally removed the bowl from the bag. If the bowl had warped only slightly I could have remounted it on the lathe, exactly as it was before, and done a bit of turning to true up the bowl.

It is important to watch a green bowl carefully while it is seasoning in a plastic bag because mold can form quickly. Some molds may discolor the wood with sap stains. If you think these stains are a plus let the molds grow, if not wipe them off with a cloth soaked in diluted vinegar and switch the bowl to a clean plastic bag.

Green-Ash Bowl

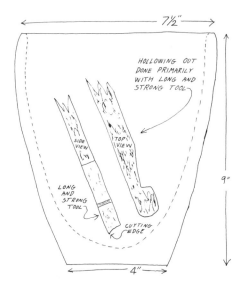

This project has two reasons for being included here. First, it is an example of a totally successful green-wood turning and, second, it was hollowed out principally with a long-and-strong tool. These sturdy tools allow a turner to safely make deep bowls of this type.

The ash log was damp with sap when I screwed it to a faceplate, engaged the dead center, and started turning. The wood cut cleanly and easily and the entire job was a joy for anyone who loves lathe work. Again I worked on the piece over a period of several days and kept it covered with two layers of plastic during the night. The Green-Ash Bowl was finished with my tung oil and carnauba wax mix and kept in a plastic bag for some additional weeks to continue seasoning.

If you try green-wood turning and like it, you might consider the purchase of one or two hooked tools which were designed for this sort of project. On some of these tools the cutting edge forms a hook while on others it is a complete circle. They are also called spiral tools because the shavings sometimes come off the cuts they make in a spiral.

Most of what I have read about green-wood turning suggests that bowls made of this material have walls of uniform thickness throughout. I have also heard this rule for turnings in general. It is a logical suggestion but I must admit that I rarely follow it. I will also admit that over the years I have had some cracked bowls, but I have had many more successes and some of the vessels that cracked were ones with uniform sides. Perhaps I tended to work with stable woods or perhaps I was just lucky, but I would say from my experience that this suggestion has limited value.

A bowl being turned in green wood.

Raw material for log turning, along with tools and a completed bowl.

Let's go back to the Fluted-Rim Bowl described in the last project. It had walls of the same thickness when it went on its warping rampage but avocado is not a stable wood so this sort of behavior is not unusual. Lastly, you may find a faster or even slower lathe speed helpful when turning green wood, but do remember to keep your tools sharp.

Natural-Walled Bowl

In the opening to this section I made mention of bowls with entire sides missing and referred to them as flaw-encrusted turnings. I can't say that these bowls are my favorites, but I do see beauty in them and feel they deserve a place here.

This project was turned from a piece of desert juniper. It displays a lot of color contrast between the sap and heart wood. The chunk of log was cut

A finished natural-sided cedar bowl (right), and a blank to be used for a similar project.

right above the stump, which accounts for its undulating sides. The bowl design is simple to allow the unique shape of the log to have its say. This bowl was turned on a small faceplate and lightly sanded but received no finishing material.

Whether you like this free-form style or not, you must admit that natural-walled bowls open up a plethora of turning options. First, there are all the stumps and weathered logs that a few years back were mainly used for firewood but are now choice lathe material. Second, there is the fact that, no matter what the final project looks like, you can call it high art. I recommended caution when selecting, mounting, and turning these odd-shaped pieces. Be sure the piece you select is sound and that the faceplate is securely engaged. Finally, wear a full face mask and watch out for flying debris.

CARVED BOWLS

Dough Trough

Countries that have traditionally looked to bread as a diet staple all seem to have come up with a long wooden container for mixing and proofing the dough. Similarly shaped wood containers were also carved in other parts of the world where they were probably used for food processing and storage. This Dough Trough is based on one I saw in Switzerland.

I didn't make this trough for use in baking bread but rather to hold potted plants. I have also seen them used to hold magazines, fireplace kindling, and an arrangement of dried flowers lying on its side. In bygone times this project would be crafted entirely with ax, adz, and chisels but I

A Dough Trough under construction. The top is sawed out and the bottom is being carved out with an inshave. Other tools shown include homemade and commercial adz, mallet, and gouge.

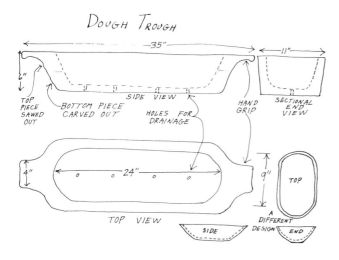

took advantage of modern technology and made the top piece of the horizontal stack with a band saw. The inside of the lower piece, however, was shaped in the traditional way. The tools I used can be seen in the photo.

The top and bottom pieces were glued together with resorcinol and the sides smoothed with plane and spokeshave. This Dough Trough-turned-plant receptacle was made from rot-resistant redwood. I drilled four holes in the bottom for drainage but I applied no finish as I wanted the project to take on that attractive weathered-redwood look.

Tsimshian Bowl

Earlier you were treated to an example of the fantastic designs of the Northwest Coast Indians in the Bentwood Box. This bowl originated in the same area but is a much less complex project. If you enjoy cutting through layer after layer of

wood to see a bowl materialize before your eyes, you will have fun making this item.

I used sycamore for this project because it imparts no taste or odor to food. The outside shape of the bowl was roughed out on the band saw and then completed with plane and spokeshave. A look at the drawing will show you that, except for the bottom, every surface on the bowl has some sort of a curve. Bent and spoon gouges proved the best tools for carving out the bowl. The inside of the bowl was sanded but faint traces of the carving marks were allowed to remain. This textured surface adds a certain design element to the Tsimshian Bowl and seemed in keeping with its origin.

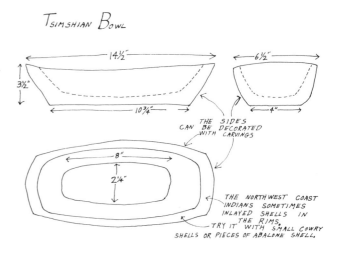

Other Northwest Coast Indians besides the Tsimshian made containers similar to this. They often decorated the outside surfaces with motifs like the ones shown on the Bentwood Box project. Many years ago I actually used this bowl to serve cooked vegetables, but now it is relegated to serving popcorn and the like.

Small Carved Bowls

Many small wooden bowls were fashioned on the American frontier where choice woods were available on every side. Glass and pottery containers were expensive and breakable so wooden bowls were put to many uses—as they can be today. The first of the two bowls illustrated has a leather loop attached and is called a noggin. It was carried on

Two Small Carved Bowls: a mesquite-root noggin with leather loop and one made from an oak burl.

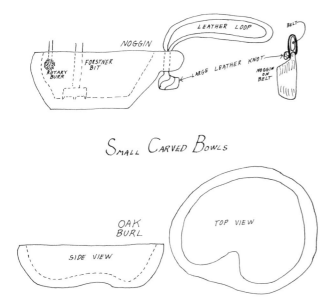

Carved Tray

Among the most popular souvenirs brought back from Hawaii or the Caribbean Islands are wooden trays shaped like tropical leaves or pieces of fruit. These trays, often carved from monkey pod wood, are certainly attractive and I encourage you to make one, but they are so well known that I would like to expose you to a different sort of tray. This tray has a rather classical look about it but apparently it was popular in Colonial America, where every utensil had to be practical and pull its own weight.

This tray was band-sawed from a 2 by 12 piece of sugar pine and then carved to shape. The carving was chiefly accomplished with large gouges to hollow out the cavity. The handles on either end offer good finger grips on the underside and an attractive shell design on the top. Note that the rim slopes in rather sharply and is concave in shape. These details are easily seen in the cross-sectional drawings. All tool marks were sanded out and the tray given a finish of walnut oil.

the belt and used to dip a drink from the pure water to be found in every lake and stream. This one was fashioned from a piece of manzanita root, which is much like French brier in that it is both hard and attractive. Noggins are made with a short handle through which the leather loop is passed. If you know anyone interested in black-powder weapons and wearing buckskins, they would likely appreciate a noggin as a gift.

The other bowl was crafted from an oak burl and can be used as a salt cellar, to serve nuts, or a desk container for paper clips or business cards. The outsides of both bowls were roughed out by saw and then smoothed with rasps and abrasive paper. The insides were hollowed out by drilling with Forstner bits and completed with rotary burrs.

If your bowl is made from a pretty wood, you may decide it needs no finish. However, if you decide to apply a finish, it should be appropriate to the planned use of the container.

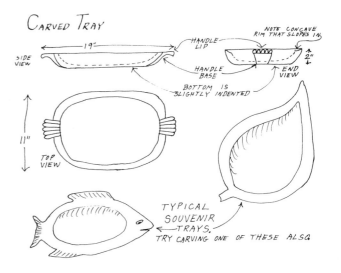

You will find many uses for a large, deep tray of this sort. Use it at breakfast to serve biscuits, muffins, or sweet rolls, at lunch to present bread, meat, and cheese, and at dinner to carry the meat, potatoes, and vegetables to the table. Made with partitions, this Carved Tray is a dandy way to present the garnishes for a curry feast. It will also function as a fruit bowl and can be hung on the wall to show off its graceful lines.

UNUSUAL BOWLS AND OTHER UNIQUE TURNINGS

Square Bowl with Forged Handles

If you looked through the projects in the boxes section, you know that I like to combine hand-made hardware with wooden items. This was a bit difficult to do here, but I managed and this bowl is the result. I started with a nice piece of red lauan 10 by 10 by 2½ inches. I sanded the end-grain sides square and planed the straight-grained

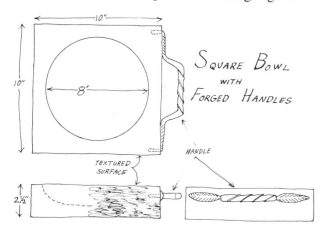

sides smooth, and then gave them a textured look with a ⅜-inch gouge.

Next, the blank was mounted on a large face-plate and a simple round depression was cut into it. Be careful when turning square blanks because those four corners can deliver a nasty blow if you get in their way. The depression was sanded smooth and the project given a coat of polyurethane.

The forged handles were made from 5/16-inch-square mild-steel stock. They are made of one piece of steel with the two ends made to look like leaves. Rather than being fastened to the bowl with handmade nails, which would detract from the leaf design, these handles have a built-in pin at the end of each leaf. These pins fit into holes in the end-grain side of the bowl along with some epoxy to ensure a secure fit. Naturally, commercial metal handles or carved wooden handles can be substituted for these forged models.

This bowl is turned only on the inside, which might make it seem like something less than an ideal lathe project, but this technique actually opens up lots of possibilities to the inventive turner. The Square Bowl with Forged Handles can be used for serving snacks or candy, as a key and change tray, or to display a collection.

Turned Piggy Bank

You may never have thought of crafting an animal body on the lathe but it's easily done and results in a clever project. I suppose other animals, like the armadillo, could be made in this manner. To me, the pig was the logical choice shapewise, besides every child needs a piggy bank.

I glued up two pieces of Philippine mahogany to form a blank and turned this between centers. The idea was to duplicate the animal's body in

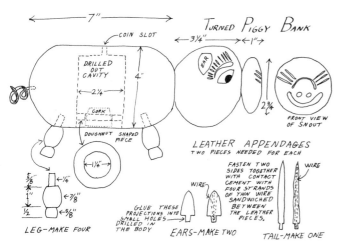

Russian Ladle

profile. Next, I turned the four short legs in maple and drilled the torso to accept these, but I did not attach them at this time. (If you fashion a very low-slung animal, like an alligator, I suggest that you saw off the lower portion of the body to make the critter stand rather than make legs.) Then drill out a portion of the body, from the bottom, to form a cavity for the bank. Cut a coin slot 1¼ inches long in the top. This is large enough to take a U.S. 50-cent piece, which is the largest coin most piggy banks will ever see. The cavity hole is plugged with a doughnut-shaped piece, the hole of which is closed with a cork.

The underside of the Turned Piggy Bank with the legs temporarily in place. Note the coin cavity with the doughnut-shaped piece glued in.

To finish the Turned Piggy Bank I first gave it a coat of sanding sealer and then two coats of oil-based enamel. The hearts-and-flowers theme and the facial features were done with acrylic enamel. I next glued in the legs and gave the entire project a coat of polyurethane. The ears and tail are made from thin leather cut as shown in the drawing. Each item requires two pieces of leather. They are put together with contact cement with thin wire sandwiched between, so the tail will curl and the ears flop.

I saw the model for this ladle many years ago at a home in British Columbia. It impressed me as having delicate lines and yet being quite practical, with the hook in the handle allowing it to be hung either inside or outside a milk pail. I was told its design came from Russia, where it was used to ladle milk, yogurt, and other dairy products.

When I returned home I was glad I had taken measurements of the ladle because I decided to make one. The wood used was well-seasoned cherry. I started by sawing out the top and side profiles of the ladle. Next, I drilled out as much wood as possible from the cavity, taking special care not to mar the inside wall of the ladle. The job of shaping and smoothing the utensil was by far the most time-consuming. I did this with carving chisels, rasps, a whittling knife, and lots of garnet paper. The finish was nut oil. My Russian ladle has always been displayed as a conversation piece, but I imagine it could be put to good use dishing out pretzels, nuts, or popcorn at a party or some similar job.

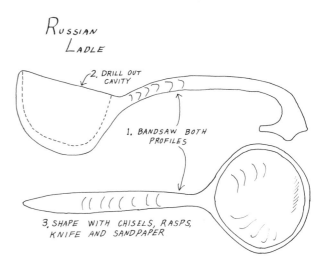

Swiss Bucket

Gluing up a bowl blank in the cooperage manner is a lot like crafting a wooden bucket so you might want to read through the opening and first project in the buckets section of this book. The basic idea is to shape some thick staves so they fit tightly around a thick bottom and flare out to form the general shape of the piece you desire to turn. A drawing in the Technical Notes of this chapter shows this.

This blank was constructed of 2-inch ash using yellow glue. My plan was to duplicate in a general way the souvenir dairy buckets I had seen in Switzerland. Just as in fabricating a bucket, the aim is for tight joints throughout. Mounting the bottom of this blank on a faceplate was easy, but how was I to bring the dead center into use with an open-ended blank? The answer was simplicity itself. I just inserted a big plug in the open end of the bucket. Next I turned the outside of the bucket round and shaped the two false hoops. Then I removed the dead center, turned the interior, and sanded the project.

To color the two false hoops I really went high tech and used brown crayon. The finish was a linseed oil and wax mixture. As the Swiss Bucket is a tall container, I see it being used to hold skewers at the barbecue, chopsticks for an Oriental meal, or bread sticks for an Italian dinner. Or how about candy sticks or pencils on a desk?

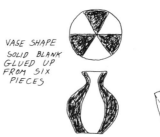

OTHER IDEAS FOR COOPERED BOWLS

VASE SHAPE SOLID BLANK GLUED UP FROM SIX PIECES

CONCAVE SIDED BOWL, HOLLOW BLANK MADE WITH EIGHT PIECES AND A BOTTOM. SECTIONAL VIEW

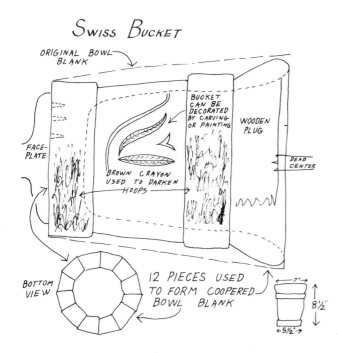

Swiss Bucket

ORIGINAL BOWL BLANK

FACE-PLATE

BROWN CRAYON USED TO DARKEN HOOPS

BUCKET CAN BE DECORATED BY CARVING OR PAINTING

WOODEN PLUG

DEAD CENTER

BOTTOM VIEW

12 PIECES USED TO FORM COOPERED BOWL BLANK

7"

8½"

5½"

Partitioned Bowl

This is perhaps the most unusual bowl in this book, yet it is an eminently practical item for

serving four snacks at once. It is also a sort of triple-talent project in that the outside is turned, the inside carved, and the false rim sawed off. The bowl blank used was glued up from 2 by 6-inch pieces of Philippine mahogany.

I started by sawing a 13-inch circle from the blank and laying out the bowl and partitions, making sure that the long grain of the wood passed through the handles. Next, I mounted a large faceplate on the top of the blank, being careful that none of the screws hit the partitions. The turning of the outside of the bowl is a simple lathe exercise. Remove the faceplate.

To hollow out the four cavities I first went to my drill press and drilled out as much wood as possible. Naturally I was careful not to dig into the sides. Next, I went to work with very sharp chisels. Spoon and bent gouges worked best for the sides while my favorite tool for the partitions was a ½-inch pattern maker's model.

Sanding the inside of the Partitioned Bowl proved rather tricky. I ended up crafting two items that made the job a lot easier. One was a sanding slat and the other a 1¼-inch leather wheel to be mounted on a mandrel and used with a rotary tool. Both were covered with 80-grit garnet paper. After the inside was completed the excess rim was cut away with a coping saw and sanded smooth, thus forming the handles. The completed bowl was darkened with a homemade brew, consisting of black walnut hulls simmered in water for an hour, and then given a coat of bowl lacquer.

Classic Greek Vase

Have you ever wanted to attach handles or a spout to a turned piece? Well I have, and the only answer I could come up with was to fasten these items to the turning after it was complete. Attaching these auxiliary pieces with a butt-glue joint left me wondering if such a joint would provide sufficient strength. It was then I remembered that I had some dowelling centers that would make it easy to fasten even small pieces to a turning. This vase is an example of that technique.

The turning blank was glued as a vertical stack from ½-inch Philippine mahogany salvaged from

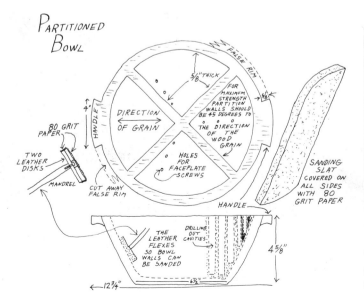

With the turning completed, this classic Greek Vase is ready for its handles. The roughed-out handles are shown along with a set of dowel centering points.

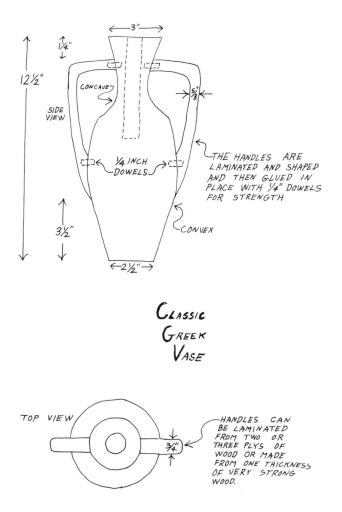

C*LASSIC* G*REEK* V*ASE*

Band-Saw Bonsai Bowl

Real aficionados of bonsai culture pot their specimens in special rectangular ceramic bowls. When I had my collection of these tiny trees some years ago, I did not have access to a supply of these bowls so, as I so often do, I decided to make my own containers. I used all heart redwood, but some of the cedars and black locust which are quite rot resistant would also do nicely. My design for the bowl was an attempt to make it as Oriental as possible.

This project was constructed from four lengths of 2 by 4-inch lumber. Almost all of the shaping is done on the band saw, working with the four pieces individually. To shape the top two pieces I

some pallets. Plan the shape you desire carefully and take pains to cut the pieces accurately because it's easy to miscalculate when gluing up a vertical stack. I squared up the ends of my blank, mounted it between faceplate and dead center, and completed the turning and sanding. I then glued four pieces of scrap together to form two handles and sawed these to shape. A few minutes of whittling and sanding and the handles were complete. Next, I drilled ¼-inch holes in the vase, inserted my dowelling centers, and marked the spots on the handles for the corresponding holes. I inserted short pieces of dowel, checked the fit, and then glued the handles in place. The vase was finished with sanding sealer and black spray paint.

So what does one do with a Classic Greek Vase? It *could* serve as a very elegant weed pot, but I see it filling a more specific need. I visualize vases of this sort, carrying nameplates and resting on pedestals, being used as sports trophies or prizes at art and craft shows.

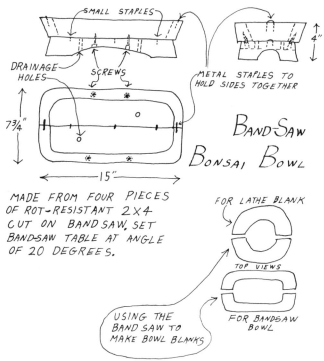

B*AND*-S*AW* B*ONSAI* B*OWL*

MADE FROM FOUR PIECES OF ROT-RESISTANT 2X4 CUT ON BAND SAW. SET BAND-SAW TABLE AT ANGLE OF 20 DEGREES.

set my band-saw table to 20 degrees and cut both the inside and the outside. This method of removing the waste from the inside of a piece for a round bowl has not been discussed but it is an excellent technique. The two pieces have only to be glued together to make a circle for a bowl blank. The inside pieces can, of course, be used to make smaller bowls.

The bottom two pieces are not hollowed out; however, the outside of each piece is tapered at the same angle as the top pieces. Then, with the band-saw table on the level, the legs are shaped. At the drill press, drill holes for drainage and to countersink the screws that hold the top and bottom together.

I used staples to attach the sides together. On the top you can use large commercial or home-crafted staples. I employed smaller commercial staples to hold the bottom pieces together. The next step is to fasten the top and bottom sections together with long wood screws. These are inserted from the underside.

I finished my Band-Saw Bonsai Bowl with a method that has wide application for boxes and buckets. This is a burn and brush system. The source of heat can be a propane acetylene or old-fashioned blowtorch or even a barbecue fire. The idea is to slightly char the surface of the bowl and then to brush out some of the charred wood with a soft wire brush. Wear tough gloves when doing this task. This process makes an attractive finish with no other coating and it marries well with the dwarf bonsai trees.

AN OLD BONSAI

Mayan Three-Legged Bowl

The Mayan civilization was one of the most advanced in the New World. They excelled at weaving, lapidary, and pottery, with many of their ceramic pieces having a tripod base. I have never seen this idea used on a turned wooden bowl, although I suspect it has been tried. This is my attempt to copy a Mayan clay pot in wood.

This bowl was made in two parts, namely a hollowed-out, bowl-like top fastened to a hollowed-out base with cutouts forming the three feet. My choice of woods was dictated by the fact that I had some thick pieces of redwood in my shop. I believe any turnable wood could be utilized. I first band-sawed two disks with a 15-degree taper on the sides. Each of these was mounted, in turn, on the same faceplate and the sides shaped and the cavity hollowed out. To assure that the small end of each piece would be the same diameter, I simply turned each down to the size of the faceplate.

After the lower part was completed on the lathe I worked up a template for the three cutouts, transferred this to the bowl, and cut out the three arch-shaped pieces with a coping saw. I used a fine-toothed blade set to cut on the pull stroke. To fasten the upper and lower parts together, I employed three wood screws. The stratagem of turning two bowl-like parts and fastening them

MAYAN THREE-LEGGED BOWL

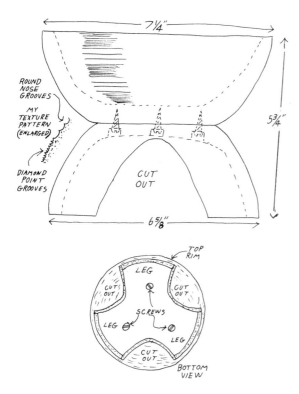

together and the cutting away of portions of a bowl's sides present all sorts of possibilities for the inventive turner. Many ideas come to mind like hexapod bowls or bowls with fretwork designs in their sides.

Each piece of this Mayan Three-Legged Bowl was given a textured finish while still on the lathe. This sort of rough finish would have been totally unacceptable some years back, when every bowl was sanded to a fare-thee-well, but now projects with this finish win prizes. It's an interesting way to complete a bowl and certainly has its place in every turner's bag of tricks. You will probably find that very sharp tools and a higher speed help when using this technique to add character to a bowl. I did my texturing in bands about ½ inch wide. One band consists of tiny grooves made with a diamond-point tool and the other is made up of three grooves formed with a round-nose tool. This arrangement was strictly a personal choice. I encourage you to experiment with your lathe tools and different woods to discover your own favorite texture treatment. For any bowl that will be handled a great deal, a light coat of clear spray finish would be a good idea.

Metric Equivalents

INCHES TO MILLIMETRES AND CENTIMETRES

MM—millimetres   *CM—centimetres*

Inches	MM	CM	Inches	CM	Inches	CM
⅛	3	0.3	9	22.9	30	76.2
¼	6	0.6	10	25.4	31	78.7
⅜	10	1.0	11	27.9	32	81.3
½	13	1.3	12	30.5	33	83.8
⅝	16	1.6	13	33.0	34	86.4
¾	19	1.9	14	35.6	35	88.9
⅞	22	2.2	15	38.1	36	91.4
1	25	2.5	16	40.6	37	94.0
1¼	32	3.2	17	43.2	38	96.5
1½	38	3.8	18	45.7	39	99.1
1¾	44	4.4	19	48.3	40	101.6
2	51	5.1	20	50.8	41	104.1
2½	64	6.4	21	53.3	42	106.7
2	76	7.6	22	55.9	43	109.2
3½	89	8.9	23	58.4	44	111.8
4	102	10.2	24	61.0	45	114.3
4½	114	11.4	25	63.5	46	116.8
5	127	12.7	26	66.0	47	119.4
6	152	15.2	27	68.6	48	121.9
7	178	17.8	28	71.1	49	124.5
8	203	20.3	29	73.7	50	127.0

Author Warren Asa enjoys "making the chips fly."

ABOUT THE AUTHOR

Warren Asa received his first tool chest when he was four years old. He didn't know how to construct anything but he enjoyed making shavings with the sharp, well-made German plane and pounding nails with the small hammer. At six he discovered a light carpentry job he could do at his father's greenhouse in Pana, Illinois, and by ten he could keep up with the adults at the greenhouse on hammer-and-saw jobs. When young Asa was twelve he joined the Boy Scouts of America and his life took on much broader horizons with campcraft, Indian lore, and the merit badge program. High school offered mechanical drawing and wood shop with power tools, an open-sesame to more varied and professional craftwork.

Service with the Army's Tenth Mountain Division and graduation from the University of Illinois widened Asa's interests. During this period, he started leading foreign bicycle trips for American Youth Hostels. On these trips he had a chance to visit many artisans and to examine their work. Although his professional career centered around horticulture, youth leadership, and teaching as a college professor, he also involved himself in less usual pursuits as a mountain guide, glacial research worker, and recreation consultant. Early in his career, Asa set up a workshop to do freelance craft writing. He sold his first article in 1951 and has been at it ever since.

Warren Asa lives with his wife, Mary Jeanne, who is an accomplished weaver, in Glendora, California. Their children, Linda, Joe, and Bonnie, all like to work with their hands in a number of disciplines.

INDEX